FARM WOODLAND
MANAGEMENT

FARM WOODLAND MANAGEMENT

Second Edition

John Blyth, Julian Evans,
William E. S. Mutch, Caroline Sidwell

FARMING PRESS

First published 1987
Second edition 1991

British Library Cataloguing in Publication Data

Farm woodland management.
  1. Forest conservation——Great Britain
  2. Forest management——Great Britain
  I. Blyth, John
  333.75′0941   SD414.97

  ISBN 0-85236-219-6

Published by Farming Press Books
4 Friars Courtyard
30–32 Princes Street
Ipswich IP1 1RJ, United Kingdom

Distributed in North America
by Diamond Farm Enterprises,
Box 537, Alexandria Bay, NY 13607, USA

Phototypeset by Galleon Photosetting, Ipswich
Printed in Great Britain by Butler and Tanner, Frome, Somerset

Contents

List of Plates

List of Figures

List of Tables

PREFACE

THIS BOOK aims to generate both interest and action. The present trends in European agricultural policy suggest that 'trees as a farm crop' will become a reality in the British countryside. We have therefore attempted to start on a relatively practical note, after an introductory look at the reasons for growing trees, with three chapters covering the management of existing woodland and the establishment of new woodland. The next three chapters extend this approach to consider the influence of woodland on the farm enterprise and the wider environment, and vice versa, including the impact of financial, fiscal and institutional considerations. The final three revert to practical guidance on timber harvesting and woodland planning at the strategic and operational levels.

Farm woodlands in Britain represent a largely neglected resource and the purpose of this book is to encourage farmers to consider their management as an integral part of overall land husbandry. Our contention, stated in Chapter 1, is 'that this can be financially and aesthetically rewarding, despite the long-term nature of the exercise, and at the same time provide opportunities for recreation and wildlife conservation.' This is equally true for new farm woodlands provided they are designed with clear objectives in mind and sensitively managed.

We would like to acknowledge permission from Mr Mike Hellewell and ADAS to use the section on managing farm hedges which is reproduced in Chapter 3, which we feel includes all that we wished to say. We gratefully acknowledge permission from the Forestry Commission to reproduce, from FC publications, Appendix 1 and several tables in Chapter 8 and to use photographs from their Edinburgh photographic library in Plates 1.1–1.12, 3.3, 8.1–8.12, and 10.1–10.10. Grateful thanks are due to the Macaulay Land Use Research Institute for permission to reproduce the diagrams used in Figure 9.2 and photographs were also kindly provided by Dr K. Stott (Plate 4.2), Henry Venables Ltd (Plate 8.4), the Nature Conservancy Council (Plate 1.4) and F. Sinclair (Plate 9.2).

Finally, our heartfelt thanks to Penny Legg, Margaret Jackson and Dave Haswell for putting up with requests for typing, photography and cartographic work at ridiculously short notice, and to Eric Todd for timely advice and information.

JOHN BLYTH
JULIAN EVANS
BILL MUTCH
CAROLINE SIDWELL   *August 1987*

Chapter 1

WHY GROW TREES?

TREES ARE a part of our national heritage. After the last ice age about ten thousand years ago pioneer species such as birch, alder, willow and pine followed the retreating glaciers northwards and as climatic conditions improved, more demanding species like oak, elm and lime became established. This natural process was halted by the formation of the English Channel about five thousand years ago so that Britain has a relatively small native tree flora of thirty-three species (only three are conifers—Scots pine, yew and juniper). Over the centuries settlers from mainland Europe have introduced other species that they knew were useful for shelter, fodder, fruit and timber such as the sweet chestnut brought by the Romans. In the last four centuries a large number of tree species have been introduced from all over the world. Examples include the European larch (about 1625), Turkey oak (about 1735) and a handful of western American conifers in the early nineteenth century of which Douglas fir and Sitka spruce have become commercially important.

If the Romans discovered a largely tree-covered landscape where have all the trees gone? The decline in woodland cover has been mainly due to clearance for agriculture, assisted by cutting for industrial uses. Although large areas including the Royal forests were retained primarily for hunting, substantial areas of woodland were managed, albeit extensively, to produce fuel, timber and a variety of products for farm and household use. The traditional management system of hazel coppice with oak standards—for sheep hurdles and building timber respectively— is a good example in medieval Britain; charcoal for smelting and the Chiltern bodgers' beech furniture are examples from later periods. Some woodland provided sheltered grazing for animals and oak was extensively coppiced for its bark (used in tanning) especially in western Britain. Indeed, almost all woodland has been subjected to human intervention in some way, with only tiny remnants of truly 'natural' woodland left (Plates 1.1–1.4).

In the twentieth century traditional management practices have

1

Plate 1.1   Native Scots pine and birch woodland, Glen Affric, Inverness-shire.

Plate 1.2   Caledonian pine, Rothiemurchus Forest, Speyside.

Examples of semi-natural woodland

Plate 1.3   Ancient Kinloch ash woods, Isle of Skye.

Plate 1.4   Mixed lowland broadleaf woodland, Cawdor, Inverness-shire.

declined dramatically and, following large-scale felling in both world wars, the emphasis has been on re-establishing a national reserve of commercial timber. Conifers have been widely used because they grow faster, are easier to work, and provide an ideal raw material for paper making and general construction which are the main uses of timber in industrialised countries today. Britain currently imports 88 per cent of her timber requirements at an annual cost of nearly £7 billion—a major reason for growing trees! Since we have only one suitable native conifer species (Scots pine) this afforestation has largely been carried out with exotics from North America and elsewhere. The resurgence of interest in native species, particularly broadleaves, reflects a shift in public opinion towards a greater awareness of the environment. There is also the recent development of agricultural surpluses in Europe, which has coincided with public demand for greater environmental sensitivity in land use practices—both in agriculture and forestry.

The purpose of this book is to encourage farmers to consider woodland management as an integral part of overall land husbandry. Small farm woods cover about one-third of a million hectares, a sixth of the total woodland in Britain, while individual trees or groups of trees represent the equivalent of another hundred thousand hectares. The management of this largely neglected resource can be financially and aesthetically rewarding, despite the long-term nature of the exercise, and at the same time provide opportunities for recreation and wildlife conservation. Lack of management leads to a reduction in value on all counts.

Types of Woodland

There are two main types of woodland—coppice and so-called 'high forest'. Coppice consists of shoots arising from stumps (or stools) which are cut on a regular cycle. Before the industrial revolution this system was widely used to supply small-diameter poles for building and fencing. Today, active coppicing is mostly restricted to sweet chestnut in south-east England where it is worked for split chestnut fencing, although there is increasing interest in the system for producing fuelwood and variable wildlife habitat. High forest refers not to the size of the trees but to woodland where the trees are derived from seed and this can have a variety of forms. At one extreme, the plantation, all trees have the same age and the wood has a uniform appearance. At the other extreme the trees may have a complete range of ages, from seedlings through to mature stems, and this uneven-aged composition creates an irregular appearance. A mixture of compatible species will increase the irregularity and many people regard the 'irregular high forest' type of woodland as particularly attractive. It does, however, demand greater skill to manage, particularly in small blocks, and it may be more practicable to aim at even-aged woods of different ages, achieving irregularity between blocks rather than within them.

In between these two extremes is a range of woodland types containing approximately even-aged groups of different sizes, and 'two-storeyed' high forest where young trees grow up under the old crop which is gradually removed. In addition there is 'coppice-with-standards' woodland in which a small number of single stem trees (the standards) are retained above coppice stools to produce some large timber. Coppice working is described in Chapter 2 and the various types of woodland are illustrated in Plates 1.5–1.8.

Value of Farm Woods

Woodlands have many uses and the first step in using them constructively is to decide the main purpose of each woodland area. There will probably be subsidiary aims also, which need to be stated in order of priority. The act of stating a set of management objectives leads on to other decisions about the appropriate type of woodland, species composition and methods of working. Possible objectives include timber production, shelter, sporting value, amenity, recreation and wildlife habitat. Encouragement is given to private forestry through various forms of grant aid (see Chapter 7) and much of the work can be carried out with existing farm resources, given suitable guidance.

The range of objectives will be considered under three main heads— amenity, conservation and production. Appearance and provision for recreation and shelter will be included in the first category.

Amenity

Farm woodlands and hedgerow trees are a significant feature of the landscape, to the general public as well as to local people, and their appearance is important from a distance as well as at close range. Small rectangular blocks of even-aged plantations are much less attractive than fewer, larger units in broad sweeping terrain, while mixed irregular woodland looks 'right' on steep land along streams or rivers which is often unsuitable for agriculture. There is broad agreement about what looks pleasing to the eye, generally expressed in terms of 'sympathy with the topography', and consideration of the size, distribution and composition of woods is particularly important because of their long-term nature. By and large, straight lines and uniformity of composition (species and tree size) should be avoided although they may have a place on completely flat land.

Plate 1.5 (*above*)
Sweet-chestnut coppice, the
Weald.

Plate 1.6 Oak standards:
this woodland was planted in
the eighteenth century and
managed as coppice-with-
standards until 1930, Loch
Lomond, Perthshire.

Woodland types

Plate 1.7 (*right*) Even-aged larch high forest, age thirty-four years, South Wales.

Plate 1.8 (*below*) Uneven-aged beech high forest: note the group of natural regeneration; large trees about ninety years old, Queen Wood, Chilterns.

Close-up appearance is important when woods are used for recreation and it is interesting to note that neglected woodland is often less attractive than suitably managed woodland for an afternoon stroll or walking the dog. Thick undergrowth, overgrown paths and fallen trees can make progress just as difficult and uninteresting as dense conifer plantations. Most people enjoy large trees they can walk between easily and are happy to accept impenetrable areas provided the large trees exist and are readily accessible. Note that young broadleaves and conifers are equally uncomfortable to walk through! So, for amenity at close range, the aims should be variety in tree size and species composition, and ease of access.

Organised recreation may be an option for some—archery in a clearing, or orienteering, or a camp site for local youth organisations. Sporting value can range from the occasional rough shoot at a weekend to intensive management for let shooting during the season. For many farmers the most commonly recognised value of woodland is shelter for stock and buildings—particularly in the hills and uplands. Grazing of stock inside woods requires careful control and is only successful on freely draining sites, but well-maintained shelterbelts can be a great asset to the stockman.

Conservation
Conservation has become a household word during the last decade and is generally applied to habitat conservation of flora and fauna. However, it can equally well refer to places of historical interest such as ancient roadways, earthworks or industrial workings, many of which occur in woods. Because woodland is the natural ecosystem for most of Britain woods can be very rich in wildlife. 'Ancient semi-natural woodland' (see reference by Peterken in Appendix 2) is the richest, and all woodland owners would be well advised to consult their local Nature Conservancy Council officer (who is often a member of the local Farming and Wildlife Advisory Group) to check if their woods contain species of particular interest. This should be done earlier rather than later because it may influence the decision on management objectives.

Woodland is very much more than just trees. It provides suitable conditions for a wide range of fungi, mosses, herbaceous and woody plants, invertebrates and larger animals, not forgetting those hidden from view in rotting stumps and below ground level. Woods are also 'alive' in a different sense, in that ecological processes are continuously at work in response to short- and long-term changes in the environment, such as wind and land drainage respectively. Because the rate of change is so slow most people do not appreciate that woods are constantly changing. The size of trees changes as seedlings grow through thicket, sapling and pole stages to become timber stems, which eventually fall (or are felled) to be replaced by natural regeneration (Plates 1.9–1.12). The range of species alters as light-demanding pioneers give way to more shade-tolerant species, and all the time there are related changes in the fauna and ground flora. Indeed, conservation in the narrow sense of preserving a particular habitat generally involves active intervention by man to arrest natural changes and preserve the status quo.

New woodland is typically less interesting to the conservationist but it represents the start of a process of environmental diversification which is bound to develop increased interest over time. In order to allow species to colonise new areas 'corridors' of woodland along streamsides or hedgerows are useful to connect the 'islands' of individual woods. Internal and external boundaries are of great importance to wildlife, because of the range of habitats they represent, and small farm woodlands are particularly valuable for conservation because of their high edge length-to-area ratio. This feature presents both a challenge and an opportunity to the woodland manager, with the possibility of designing a multi-purpose edge which satisfies a range of management objectives.

Production

This is primarily of timber in one form or another but also of non-timber products. Well-managed deciduous woodland in lowland Britain grows at 5–10 cubic metres (tonnes) per hectare per year and conifers at two or three times that rate, depending on site conditions. This can be harvested in a variety of forms from small-sized roundwood for fencing, pulpwood and fuelwood to high-quality sawlogs for square-edged material or veneer. There are special uses for small material (e.g. walking-sticks) and for large trees (e.g. dock timbers), and local or specialised markets are often more valuable than the larger bulk markets such as chipboard or pallet wood. There is a growing demand for firewood in many rural areas and farmers are well placed to provide the sustained quantity and quality required. There are also non-timber woodland products such as bark, foliage for floral displays, edible fruits and fungi, and Christmas trees. There is no reason why deer, rabbits and gamebirds should not be included in this category.

Timber production from small farm woodlands can suffer from high unit costs of harvesting operations, typically due to difficult access and the small quantities offered for sale at any one time and place. This is unfortunate because farm woods often occupy fertile, sheltered sites capable of producing high-quality timber at relatively good growth rates compared with British forests as a whole. However, provided care is taken in growing the trees, and equal care in selling them, farm timber

Plate 1.9   Oak seedling emerging from tree shelter, Northamptonshire.

Stages in tree development

Plate 1.10   Thicket stage Corsican pine, age eleven years, E. England.

Plate 1.11 Pole-stage oak, age thirty-six years, near Welshpool.

Plate 1.12 Timber-stage ash, age fifty-four years, Northamptonshire: note that the fork in the central tree is high enough to obtain a valuable butt log of sports-quality timber.

can still represent a useful financial asset. According to the survey in England and Wales carried out by the Dartington Institute in 1986, woodland on the farms investigated had an average standing value of £450 per hectare and one-third of the woods were of no value to a merchant. By contrast, a mature stand of well-managed broadleaves or conifers was worth five to ten thousand pounds per hectare. So it is worth looking after a tree crop, even if the production period is a long one, and it is also worth growing quality timber—especially with broadleaves—because of the substantial price differential. It is possible to burn walnut or cherry suitable for cabinet-making (worth perhaps £500 per tonne) but you cannot make firewood into veneers!

Psychological rewards
The rewards of woodland work are as diverse as the objectives people have for growing trees, and woodland can enhance the quality of life for local populations and visitors as well as owners. But there is also a psychological reward of working with trees, involving as it does physical labour, living organisms and the art of creating the type of woodland desired—pitting one's skill against the vagaries of nature. The work involved in woodland maintenance is mostly small-scale and best done on a little-and-often basis, like gardening, which can readily be fitted into the farm work schedule. A regular weekend stroll will notice the unstocked area which needs replanting, the area of bracken where the young trees need an extra weeding, the promising ash or oak sapling among a rash of sycamore regeneration which needs protection or release from competition, the superior form of beech in one corner of the wood which would repay pruning, or the faster growth rate in another corner which could take an early thinning. Rules of thumb are better than nothing but management by the book can never be so enjoyable as personal involvement and decision making.

Woods for Farms

There does not appear to be a suitable silvic equivalent to 'horses for courses' but the point can still be made that the type of farm woodland should be appropriate to the farming system in which it is found. In the first instance this relates to site conditions. Just as farming systems and methods reflect regional and local differences in climate and soils so must the trees, and small woodland owners have the advantage of being able to recognise local site variation in their choice of species and woodland type. But in addition, woods should be considered as an element of the landscape, a habitat for wildlife and a productive component in the overall land-use pattern. Many farm woods will be located in a predominantly agricultural landscape, occupying land unsuitable for cultivation or grazing by reason of its poor drainage, steep gradient or low fertility. In such cases the decision on where to place the woodland boundary will be relatively simple. Production will probably be secondary to amenity and conservation value, with linking hedgerows and specially treated headlands to enhance the latter, and a mixed irregular type of woodland will be needed to maintain a permanently wooded appearance.

On poorer grades of land such as heath and moor, or where the planting of substantial areas of farmland is being considered, larger blocks of woodland may be appropriate and the decision on the location of boundaries is less easy. They must be related to topographic units to fit into the landscape but they must also take due consideration of wildlife habitats and be related to farming activities to fit into the farm plan. Woodland might be located for maximum shelter to assist grazing management, for example, or to make best use of farm roads. Large blocks have greater potential for production and profit, although edge zones can still be specially managed for amenity and conservation, and even-aged stands with a limited range of species may not be out of place.

The concept of establishing farm woods on former arable land is part of the present government policy to take some of Europe's surplus agricultural land out of food production. If successful, such woodland will help to maintain rural populations and, in the long term, create a woodland reserve that can provide them with a sustained livelihood.

Finally there is the possibility of agroforestry systems, the intimate integration of agriculture and forestry or, more simply, 'trees in fields'. Despite the recent upsurge of interest this concept is not new: growing beans under poplar, for example, was not uncommon in parts of southwest England in the 1940s. Research has still to show if the development of agroforestry is a practical proposition under British conditions but it is a fitting topic with which to close this introductory chapter. Why?—because it exemplifies the successful management of trees as part of farming practice.

References for Further Reading

See Appendix 2.

Chapter 2

WHAT TO DO WITH EXISTING WOODS

A Neglected Asset

THE STOCK of woodlands on farms in Britain is considerable. Woodlands of less than ten hectares in extent cover more than 350,000 hectares and there are a further 250,000 hectares of clumps and lines of trees; the bulk of this timber resource occurs on farms. Though substantial in extent it is equally true that the great majority are neglected or under-used, and are thus a wasting asset (Plate 2.1). Though trees may continue to grow each year long periods of neglect are harmful—poor trees of little value compete with good ones for growing space, salvage opportunities of diseased ones may be lost, gaps in the wood may be colonised by unwanted growth and may exacerbate wind and snow damage, and an opportunity for earning income is lost.

It is common for more than three-quarters of all small woodlands to be in this state of neglect and yet, as the study by the Dartington Trust has shown for the scattered woodlands on the culm soils of Devon, management would, on average, increase farmers' incomes by six per cent. Also, it is clear that neglect is not mainly due to an inherently poor quality of the woodland or the trees but simply to the fact that most owners do not really know what needs to be done or what can be done. In a study of neglected woods by the Countryside Commission, more than 80 per cent were judged to have some standing value, i.e. the trees were saleable where they stood, and many contained good stems exhibiting excellent growth rates. Indeed, many lowland woods are on soils which are the envy of foresters, and poor productivity should be very much the exception.

A second illustration of neglect is the fact that more than half all lowland woods were once regularly coppiced, a practice which declined in the last century and rapidly dwindled after the First World War. Coppicing, with its associated richness of fauna and flora, supplies small

14

Plate 2.1   Neglected woodland containing marketable trees.

wood products and has been the dominant management system since medieval times; yet today it is confined to less than 40,000 hectares or hardly one-eighth of what was once worked and what was the principal architect of Britain's woodland landscape.

Realising the potential of existing farm woods is rewarding: a neglected part of the farm is brought into production, an asset is made to earn its keep, and long-forgotten skills are re-acquired in the working life of the countryside.

Assessing Woods on the Farm

Getting to know one's woods and finding what they contain and what potential they have is the first important step, a step which is informative, enjoyable and often financially rewarding too. A straightforward step-by-step guide will be found in the free ADAS/Forestry Commission series *Practical Work in Farm Woods*, leaflet 2 (P3018)—'Woodland Survey and Assessment'.

Differing Needs

It was pointed out in the first chapter that farm woodlands serve many purposes. Indeed, the farmer is often the first to appreciate the value of winter shelter, sporting interest or a ready source of firewood, or an attractive feature on the land but it is perhaps harder to gauge whether a wood is of much timber value. Noting down these different benefits is the first step in assessing a woodland, and deciding which ones are most valued and are to be retained or enhanced is essential for setting management priorities. For instance, if winter shelter is paramount clearfelling of trees will generally be avoided, unless other cover is available. More selective felling of trees will be carried out when timber is wanted or regeneration must begin.

Size

Knowing the area of a wood or group of woodlands, and hence being able to estimate quantity of standing timber, is important because economies of scale apply as much in forestry as in other industries. If timber is to be sold an absolute minimum quantity can be stipulated. A buyer is unlikely to purchase timber unless he can make up a lorry load, i.e. at least 10 tonnes or preferably 20 tonnes. Ten tonnes of timber will be produced by a clump of three to four large oak trees, eight to twelve mature conifers and anything from twenty to a hundred or more pole-size thinnings. Estimating quantities of wood is described later and the more exact requirements of measuring timber for sale are described in Chapter 8.

Size is, of course, more complex than simply knowing whether a lorry load of timber can be obtained; it includes a calculation of what proportion of the farm is under woodland. The national average is around 4–5 per cent, but many believe that 7–10 per cent is nearer the ideal to provide cover, shelter and wood products for the farm business. Size also influences how one views a woodland, its potential for sustained production, possible fencing needs, amount of planting, thinning etc. Well-stocked broadleaved woodlands typically grow at an average rate of four to ten tonnes of new wood per hectare per year over a rotation, and conifers about twice as much—interesting data to compare with cereal and potato yields!

For management purposes woods can be grouped into three sizes.

1. Very small woodlands of less than one hectare are best treated as a whole entity. Two or three parts can be managed to satisfy different objectives such as yield of timber, game cover and amenity, but it is probably safest to undertake all operations over the whole wood at one time.

2. Woodlands of one to five hectares allow some subdivision into separate units, so that a five-hectare wood could be divided into as many compartments. In ideal circumstances it might be possible to work one compartment each year but usually other factors intervene in this orderly arrangement.

3. Woods over five hectares are best divided into compartments for working.

Other Woodland Values

Woodlands are a farm asset but their value may go far beyond the farm boundary. In particular woodlands may be a key landscape feature or of important conservation interest. Such rôles add interest to the woodland and may influence management practice to maintain or even enhance them. Identifying these other values should form part of woodland assessment. Assessment of amenity value, including landscape and recreational importance, will usually be reasonably self-evident but the following points should be borne in mind.

- Is the farm (and its woodlands) in a special location such as an Area of Outstanding Natural Beauty (AONB), National Park, or an Environmentally Sensitive Area (ESA)? These designations are described in Chapter 6.

- Have the woodlands or trees already been identified as a local amenity by designation of a Tree Preservation Order (TPO—explained in Chapter 7)? The District Council planning office and Forestry Commission Forest District office retain complete records.

- Has their conservation value been recognised through designation of a Site of Special Scientific Interest (SSSI), nature reserve (national or local), or informally through interest by a local naturalists' group?

In addition some kinds of woodlands where it is known that the land has been wooded since medieval times (defined as from before 1600) are generally considered important for conservation. These woods, called ancient woodlands, usually possess a rich variety of wildlife including many plants only capable of living in the woodland environment such as oxlips and lily of the valley. The presence of such plants does not prove the woodland site to be ancient but it is indicative, as is, for example, the occurrence of small-leaved lime and wild service trees. A register of ancient woodlands has been compiled by the Nature Conservancy Council and is available from them; copies are also held by County Planning officers. It is important to establish the status of a wood, because of its interesting conservation potential, and because management should be sensitive to this value.

• Occasionally woodlands contain features of archaeological interest. The more important ones are shown on Ordnance Survey maps as ancient monuments, but unusual ground patterns, ditches and other earthworks will all be of local interest. Indeed, woodlands bounded by a ditch and mound, often surmounted by a hedge, are almost certainly ancient in the above sense since it was common to throw up such an earthwork around woods in the middle ages.

Access

Ease of access to and within a woodland influences management. Although woodland operations are infrequent, good vehicular access for the transport of equipment and materials and to facilitate extraction of produce, is a great advantage. Unfortunately, many woods occur on steep slopes, in inaccessible corners or in wet areas ill-suited to farming, and access both to and within the wood is poor.

Harvesting and extracting produce is an expensive operation and having to drag logs a long way to a lorry loading point or where they are to be converted for use adds considerably to the cost. Typically, in 1989 such extraction adds £0.60 per tonne of timber per 100 metres of distance travelled. A remote wood will attract poorer prices than one well served by tracks and roads. Moreover, dragging logs over fields to reach a road, almost always a winter job, leads to soil compaction and rutting even if the contractor only works during periods of dry weather.

Within a wood, tracks and rides not only facilitate working but add greatly to its sporting and conservation potential. Wide rides open to the sky encourage wildlife and provide warm, sheltered conditions for pheasant and deer alike.

Evaluation of access should include the following factors among others:

- distance to nearest road

- provision of turning point for lorries

- whether access is all-weather or fair-weather only

- steepness of slope and rockiness of ground in the wood

- the availability of internal access routes.

If access is found to be poor and other farm developments planned are such that it will remain so, an objective of sustained timber production for a small woodland of less than five hectares should be reconsidered. Greater priority could be given to other purposes such as shooting cover, amenity and conservation, although wood could be cut occasionally to fit in with the use of neighbouring land or when equipment is at hand.

One other access consideration is the presence of public rights of way such as paths and bridleways. The presence of these will influence management. Due care will be needed to ensure safe working practices, as with normal farm operations in a public place, but, in forest work it will sometimes be necessary to warn of operations taking place and even to explain them since they may be unfamiliar. Countless times, the revival of the ancient and conservation-benefiting practice of coppicing is mistaken for land clearing with all the environmental outcry that that incurs!

Woodland Condition

Assessing the condition and quality of the woodland itself is quite straightforward and, in practice, differs little from viewing an arable crop. The basic questions to answer are: what is the crop; how well stocked is the ground; what stage has the crop reached (age); is it of high quality; and is it healthy?

Composition

The tree species present are an important factor affecting potential uses, values and profitability. Most woodlands have several tree species but generally either conifers or broadleaves will be dominating. Intimately mixed woods are uncommon, though in larger woods it is quite common for different parts or compartments to be dominated by different species.

Not every species present needs to be noted for management purposes, but for each working area all species which make up more than twenty per cent of the crop should be recorded. In the case of conifers classification into pines, spruces, larches, Douglas fir and 'other' will usually be more than sufficient. Although there are significant differences in potential markets and end uses (see Appendix 1) the treatment of all conifer species is much the same.

This is not so with broadleaves. Coppice crops are treated very differently from stands managed for timber. The simple statistic of rotation length will vary, for example, from just a few years for some coppice systems, to twenty or thirty years for poplars and willows, to forty to eighty years for ash, cherry and sycamore, and up to two hundred years or more for oak. Similarly the relative importance of quality and how to improve it varies from very small in coppice systems to high when, for example, growing good crops of oak, ash and beech for timber.

Where a crop is of more than one species (mixed) the main decision to take is which trees to grow on the longest and form the final crop. These trees will have to be sufficiently favoured in thinning to prevent them being overtopped or dominated by others. This is a common problem with conifer:broadleaved mixtures where, especially on fertile sites, the more rapid growth of the conifer can too easily begin to dominate. In commercial woodlands it is often desirable to favour one species but if the aim is to maintain a mixed woodland, thinning should be carried out to favour the best stems irrespective of species. The forester's tool of thinning out the crops at intervals can thus control the composition of species: in a typical lowland wood most of the common sallows and birches would perhaps be removed, the better ash and oak favoured for timber and any field maples and wild service left for conservation. A fuller account of thinning is considered later in this chapter.

Stocking
The density of tree cover indicates whether the ground is being underused (Plate 2.2) or whether there is overstocking and trees are becoming drawn up. By implication this shows the urgency of such operations as thinning.

There are many tables and guides to stocking but a useful rule of thumb is that after the thicket stage, spacing between trees should be about one-fifth of average height for younger stands and one-quarter for older ones nearer maturity. Substantial departure from these proportions will indicate serious under- or overstocking.

Plate 2.2 Open, poor-quality woodland in Kent, of little value for browsing or shelter and even less for forestry with livestock eating any regeneration, barking trees and compacting the soil on this wet site.

Age

In most woodlands trees in one area or stand will be of similar age. Knowing the age will help indicate how many years there are to final felling, the rate of growth, whether the stand is already overmature (Plate 2.3), and so on. Often local records are available to show the year of planting or regeneration. If these records are not available, rings can be counted on a stump of a representative felled tree.

The main stages through which a stand goes are shown in Table 2.1.

Health and vigour

Stand health and vigour are closely related but, in general, few diseases and pests cause wholesale deaths or a moribund state. Most ill-health in trees occurs in individuals or small groups. Signs to look for include crown dieback, fungal brackets on stem, defoliation, bleeding from bark, and small, pale or yellow leaves. A consultant's help should be sought if more than 5 per cent of main crop trees exhibit such symptoms.

The rate at which trees grow varies enormously depending on species, site conditions, climate, and incidence of damage. Even in one stand,

Plate 2.3   Over-mature beech woodland in the Peak district. Broken wall long ago allowed access to sheep which effectively denies any possibility of tree seedling regeneration or growth of cover for game.

unless all trees are of one clone as in a poplar plantation, there will be considerable variation in vigour with, typically, some trees more than thirty per cent bigger and some more than thirty per cent smaller than the average. A general assessment of vigour can be made by using the Yield Class system (Chapter 8) which classifies stands based on height:age relationships. For most general management purposes knowledge of yield class, though helpful, is not essential and decisions can be based on current conditions, noting such factors as stocking, health and average tree size. Two simple indications of vigour are length of current shoots and width of recent annual rings. If either is showing marked decline—shortening or narrowing—in the last few years compared with ten or more years previously this may indicate ill-health, underthinning, overmaturity or other adverse conditions.

Quality
Quality in stands being grown for timber is judged by the proportion of defect-free, straight stems. In conifers most stems are straight but

Table 2.1. Development of a stand grown for timber, by age, size and stocking

Stage	Age (years)	Mean tree size height (m)	diameter (cm)	Typical stocking (stems per ha)
Establishment	0–10	0–5	0–6	1,000–3,000+
Thicket	5–20	2–10	4–12	1,000–2,000
Pole stage				
early thinning	15–50	8–18	7–25	500–1,000
late thinning	30–100+	15–30+	20–50+	150–600
Mature	40–150+	18–30+	30–60+	70–300
Overmature as timber	over 80 years for most conifers; over 100 years for ash, sycamore and wild cherry; over 200 years for beech and 250 years for oak			

Note: (1) vigorous stands will reach stages in growth earlier than slower-growing ones; (2) most conifers are considered mature when 20–25 m high and 30–40 cm diameter; for oak and beech larger size is sought, at least 50 cm diameter; (3) the diameter of a tree is, by convention, measured at 1.3 m height above the ground, and is often referred to as diameter at breast height (DBH).

quality is downgraded by 'defects' of heavy branching, damage to stem and, sometimes, excessively fast growth which leads to wide annual rings (more than 1 cm). In broadleaves, assuming healthy, defect-free stems, the principal criterion of quality is length of straight stem. In both types of stand, thinning is the tool used to improve quality by removing poorer trees and encouraging the better ones.

History

It is not only interesting but instructive to know the early history of older woodlands, especially establishment, since this will assist current management, indicate what silviculture has been practised (and been successful in view of the stand before you!), and some of the options available. A lot can be learnt about a woodland by interpreting what is observed or has been recorded during the assessment. Some commoner indicators are:

- The presence of an occasional conifer in a predominantly broadleaved woodland is a good indication that the woodland was originally a mixture. The conifers probably acted as a 'nurse' for the broadleaves and were mostly removed in early thinnings.

- Many shoots growing up from individual stumps is a result of coppicing, a very common practice up to forty or fifty years ago but now largely confined to sweet chestnut in south-east England. Where coppice is observed it is almost always safe to resume the practice, even after many years' neglect, to supply firewood, poles, posts, etc.

  Often there are larger trees scattered among the coppice; these are standards and are grown to provide timber.

- Any evidence of straight lines—trees lined up in rows even if now there are many gaps—usually indicates the stand was planted.

- Early Ordnance Survey maps will show if the land was woodland in the first part of the last century and will be suggestive, or otherwise, as to whether it is an ancient woodland site.

- Concentrations or pockets of different species through a woodland frequently reflect changing soil conditions as foresters of an earlier generation sought to match species with site to a degree not often now practised. Conversely, markedly uneven growth across a pure stand may indicate where the species planted was ill-suited. It may show where remedial measures of better site preparation—cultivation or drainage—or fertiliser input were needed or were inadequately carried out.

Lessons learned from how the present crop has grown greatly help both with determining what to do with the crop itself and what to do for a successor. The rest of the chapter considers the principal options available in handling existing woodlands, the kinds of operations there are and how they are carried out.

Woodland Operations—Treatment in Relation to Need

Thinning

Thinning is a powerful tool which the forester uses to bring his final crop to its best possible condition (Plate 2.4). Most forests begin with 1,000–2,500 trees per hectare but finish up with between 70 and 350 at the end of the rotation. Effecting this reduction during the life of the crop is thinning. There is nothing mysterious about the operation and it can be likened to thinning out in a seedbed when weak, unhealthy seedlings are culled both because they are poor themselves and to give more growing space to the remainder.

The practical work of thinning—cutting and extracting the trees—is usually carried out by a contractor who should have the proper equipment for safe working. However, marking which trees to cut can, of course, be done by the owner, agent or the contractor—though the latter should be well supervised as there is the continual temptation to take the best trees! Marking the thinnings in one's own wood is satisfying and the outline below is designed to help the owner do this.

If more than a few trees are to be thinned a felling licence will be required from the Forestry Commission—see page 114.

When to thin?

In a normally stocked woodland the first thinning takes place when trees reach an average height of eight to nine metres. If initial spacing was wide—more than two metres apart—thinning might be delayed until trees are about ten metres tall. Delaying thinning beyond this time will cause trees to be drawn up with small crowns, slender weak stems and crowded roots; when they are thinned they will be more at risk from wind and snow damage.

In the mid-life of a crop the need to thin is judged from the spacing between trees using the rule of thumb given earlier (page 20). Generally, in growing trees for a timber crop they should neither be kept so close that crowns are small and restricted to a tuft at the top of a long slender

Plate 2.4   Thirty-year-old sweet chestnut stand in Essex after two thinnings.

stem nor kept so open that crowns are barely touching one another and grow down almost to ground level with heavy branches. Where thinning has begun at the right time further thinnings are carried out at about five-yearly intervals for the first two or three thinnings in young crops; then at six- to eight-year intervals for later thinnings. Oak and beech grown on long rotations are thinned every ten years or so after the age of about eighty years.

It would of course be possible, even ideal for the well-being of the crop, to thin out some trees every year, but such intensive treatment is expensive because few trees are removed at any one time. The intervals recommended above are a compromise between maximising the quantity of produce at each thinning and not lengthening the interval to such an extent that the thinning itself, being necessarily so heavy, places the crop at great risk as it is opened up.

Which trees to mark and how many?
At first thinning in dense stands, particularly of conifers or the conifer component of a mixture, the removal of every third or fourth row of trees is a simple way to thin—see Plate 2.5. It reduces the stocking and provides more growing space for the remaining trees but does not lead to any quality improvement for the stand. Also on wet sites in exposed locations such line thinning increases the risk of windthrow and should be avoided.

In later thinnings and in all broadleaved stands a more selective approach to thinning should be followed. Trees should be chosen for removal—thinned out—in the following order of priorities.

1. Trees which are dead, dying, diseased or otherwise defective.

2. Trees with forks, multiple leaders or unstraight stems.

3. Trees of undesirable species which interfere with main crop ones.

4. Any poorer, slower-growing trees or tall whippy, slender ones among tight groups whose removal will lead to more even spacing throughout the crop.

5. Any other trees interfering with the best stems favoured for the final crop.

Of course, if all the trees in the above categories were removed at any one thinning, this might be excessively heavy, but the principle remains for all thinnings—remove the poorest to favour the best.

Assuming the above thinning intervals, one should aim to remove about one-quarter of all trees each time for the first few thinnings (Plate

Plate 2.5   Mixed crop of pine and beech in Hampshire, age twenty-nine years, originally planted in alternating three-row-wide bands of each species. One row in three of the pine has been thinned out and good stems of beech have been marked as potential final crop trees to be favoured in subsequent thinnings.

2.5) and about one-third each time in later thinnings. A typical life-history for a conifer crop starting with two thousand trees per hectare is shown in Table 2.2.

Final felling may be brought forward for many reasons, but the above steady reduction in tree numbers illustrates what happens to a stand. In

Table 2.2. Typical development of a conifer stand through the thinning stages

Thinning	Height (m)	Age (years)	Stocking after thinning (trees/ha)	Produce
First	9	15–25	1500	pulpwood
Second	11–14	20–30	1100	pulp/fenceposts
Third	14–17	25–40	800	pulp/posts/logs
Fourth	17–21	35–50	550	posts/small logs
Fifth	22–25	40–60	350	posts/small logs
Final felling	25–30+	45–75		sawlogs

broadleaved stands a similar pattern would take place, though in long-rotation crops, where larger-size beech or oak trees are grown, final stocking would be reduced to 80–200 trees per hectare after several more thinnings.

The actual marking of the trees to be thinned (i.e. the ones to be cut) is done by axe to blaze either side of the stem or by a dab or spray of paint, which has the advantage of allowing second thoughts.

In the case of broadleaves, where there are usually relatively few good-quality trees, it is best to identify the good ones first, say 300–400 of the best stems per hectare (Plate 2.5), and to mark them in some clear way that does not harm the trees—and is different from the thinning mark! Then, when marking the thinning, these good trees can easily be located and favoured by being given room to grow.

Yield from thinning
The amount of produce yielded in thinning varies mainly with crop vigour and the interval between thinnings, but for average conifer crops thinned on a five-year cycle, about 30–60 cubic metres per hectare can be expected each time. For slower-growing broadleaves the figure will be about half this amount.

Pruning

Little pruning is carried out in modern British forestry because of uncertainty that it will pay in higher prices for the timber. There are two main purposes: to produce a single stem (more commonly in broadleaves) and to produce knot-free wood (especially in conifers). The operation is costly and must be started when the tree stems are small, in order to restrict the core of knotty wood and allow many years of clear wood to be laid down. It must be done carefully, cutting branches cleanly without damaging the bark of the main stem. (NB. I do not support the pruning of side branches from hardwoods.)

Side branches may be cut from young conifers, especially pine, larch and Douglas fir, in two or even three 'lifts' or stages, usually associated with successive thinnings; the objective being to create a long knot-free bole without reducing the live crowns of these selected trees. Only the best trees per hectare should be pruned and never to more than half their current height.

Pruning to produce single-stemmed broadleaves and knot-free conifers is more likely to be worth-while in lowland farm woods than in upland low-input forests, because of the better opportunities for high quality timber production offered by farm woods. Pruning is sometimes needed to make trees safe, especially next to roads, tracks and buildings.

Final Felling and Regeneration

All woodlands will reach a stage when they have to be regenerated. This will occur naturally over long periods if the woodland is simply abandoned, but normally a stage is reached when the crop is finally felled, revenue obtained, and regeneration commenced. It is an important stage, bringing in the bulk of all income earned from growing trees and being the one opportunity when a change in species and woodland composition can be made. Opportunities to change land use from forest to farm land or building development will be rare, and the issue of a felling licence for clearfelling is usually conditional on a requirement to replant or regenerate naturally. (See p. 113 for more information on felling.)

When to carry out final felling

In general a stand is felled when the bulk of the trees reach a size suitable for sale as sawlogs. For conifers this is an average stem diameter of at least twenty-five centimetres and for broadleaves, including slower-growing oak and beech, forty-five or more centimetres, though in this latter case stands are often grown on for longer to even larger size. Typical final felling ages (rotations) for conifers are 40–70 years, for fast-growing broadleaves (ash, sycamore, wild cherry and sweet chestnut) 50–90 years and for oak and beech 100–180+ years.

Other factors such as a desire to grow large, impressive trees for their attraction, overmaturity, risk of windthrow, the price:size relationship for the species concerned, or need for capital (perhaps to invest in other developments on the farm), may influence the timing of final felling. It is best to seek advice on this important decision which realises the accumulated asset a woodland stand represents.

How to carry out final felling

In Britain most stands are clearfelled; that is, all the trees on a site are felled at the same time. This is the cheapest way but obviously brings the biggest change to the site, from trees to no trees virtually overnight. Clear felling is acceptable where there is little landscape or amenity importance but may be less suitable where amenity considerations are to the fore, such as stands adjacent to public rights of way or which are attractive hillside features. In such situations it may be possible to thin heavily and underplant with shade-tolerant species, removing the overstorey when the young trees are established after 5 to 10 years. The retention of even a small number of mature trees on the perimeter of the area can make a major contribution to landscape amenity. If natural regeneration is hoped for (that is the present crop of trees are to be the parents of the next), the felling should be taken in two or three stages over several years. The aim will be to provide enough seed and give some shelter to the newly emerging seedlings, creating for a time a two-storey forest—mature trees and young regrowth.

When seeking advice on when to fell, the options for regeneration should also be considered. In general non-native conifers—spruces, firs and larches—cannot be relied on to regenerate naturally, though there are exceptions depending mainly on site conditions. However, most broadleaves will regenerate naturally if the timing of operations is carefully controlled to coincide with good seed years, and some species such as ash, birch and sycamore regenerate very freely. Natural regeneration generally better serves the interests of nature conservation, providing, of course, that it is successful, which requires suitable ground conditions for seed germination and seedling development as well as a good seed year.

The safest way to re-establish a woodland is to fell and replant, but other options should always be considered.

The special regeneration system of coppice is described below and establishment by planting, whether new afforestation or replanting a felled woodland, is described in Chapter 4.

Coppice

Coppice is a way of treating woodlands to produce regular quantities of small or pole-size products and using the regrowth of shoots from the cut stump for the next crop (Plate 2.6). It was widely practised in the middle ages to produce firewood, wattle for building and other stick and pole products but today the practice is confined to sweet chestnut in south-

Plate 2.6 Two-year-old coppice shoots springing from stump of sweet chestnut, Kent.

east England and small areas of hazel and mixed coppices worked mainly for the conservation of wildlife and, indeed, the perpetuation of rural tradition. However, there is a resurgence of interest in coppicing as a simple method of management, of desirable conservation value and for supplying firewood. All broadleaved species, with the exception of beech in drier, eastern counties, can be managed as coppice.

Coppice is worked on cutting cycles of eight to thirty years depending on species and product. The whole crop is cut and the stump regrowth recruited as the next crop. Apart from possibly some initial protection from animals—livestock and deer especially—little needs to be done to a coppice crop. The rapid regrowth from the stumps quickly overcomes any competing weeds while the numerous shoots produced are either allowed to thin themselves naturally, or are reduced to two or three per stool.

There are substantial areas of neglected coppice, especially in the English lowlands, of which a large proportion are farm woods. The commonest type is over-mature hazel with oak standards—scattered large oaks with an understorey of old hazel with stems far too thick for thatching spars or bean sticks. Many other woods are old mixed coppices where all broadleaved species were worked together as coppice, typically ash, oak, wild cherry, alder, field maple, lime, willows, etc. It is clear that even after sixty or seventy years of neglect coppicing can be resumed in all types of crop except hazel. Hazel dies after about forty years and, even if it is still alive (has been coppiced at least once since the last war), the demand for its product is very localised, though there has been something of a rise in demand in recent years to satisfy the increased interest in thatching.

If one does not wish to resume coppicing it is usually possible to thin out stems on a stump (eventually to a single stem) to grow on to tree size. This is called storing coppice (Plate 2.7).

The conservation value of coppice lies in the regular influx of light to the woodland floor which encourages profuse growth of woodland plants. Most coppice woodlands have a varied structure of crops at several different stages and nearly all of them have always been woodland sites (i.e. are ancient), and are therefore a link back to the woodland flora of ancient Britain. The factors which confer desirable conservation benefits are also of value to field sports. Small copses (coppices) are ideal cover for foxes and patches of coppice within a woodland make useful flushing points for game birds.

Working coppice

Working small areas of coppice, perhaps as a local source of firewood, is one of the forest operations well suited to the farmer or owner with the

Plate 2.7   Eighteen-year-old coppice of sycamore. In this instance the coppice will not be cut in the normal way but the best stems (marked) will be left to grow on to produce timber. This is called storing coppice.

proper equipment and adequate training in safe working practices and is winter work. The crop consists of small-size stems easily handled by the smallest, lightweight chainsaws and is best extracted by tractor and trailer. Heavy saws and direct tractor extraction of logs are not required.

Coppices of native broadleaves, except for hazel, yield about 80–100 tonnes of freshly felled wood (40–60 tonnes air-dry) per hectare every twenty to twenty-five years. Typical house heating requirements are for about eight tonnes (dry) per year so four to five hectares of coppice could supply fuelwood needs in perpetuity cut at the rate of about one-quarter hectare per year. Coppices of fast-growing broadleaves such as poplars, willows, eucalypts and southern beech (*Nothofagus* spp.) are two to three times as productive and could be worked on a shorter rotation (say ten years).

Establishing a new coppice does not differ from other forms of planting discussed in Chapter 4 except that spacing should be about three metres and a first cut of stick-size material taken when trees are about five to seven centimetres in diameter to initiate the first coppice crop from the stumps. If after coppicing not all stumps sprout, whether in new or long-established coppices, make good any gaps more than five metres across by planting a tree in the middle.

Improving Poor-quality Woodland

'Poor quality' is partly a subjective idea. Open woodland with few marketable species is poor for timber production but may be of inestimable value for conservation; similarly a mature stand of beech with little undergrowth and draughty conditions may be a fine crop but poor for game. Deciding the main purpose for the woodland will help determine whether or not it is 'poor'. Nevertheless, if the intention is to grow timber there are three characteristics which commonly downgrade woodland condition: (1) low stocking with large gaps between potential timber trees; (2) low density of marketable species—woodland dominated by thorns, elder, dogwood, hazel, sallows etc.; and (3) badly tended woodland with much undergrowth, climbers, fallen or leaning trees from past storms.

Enrichment

Enrichment is the planting of additional trees in gaps to improve the stocking of thicket stage on older crops (Plate 2.8). In gaps with an effective diameter of more than one and a half times the height of adjacent trees, new planting, or the favouring of any regeneration present with adequate protection and cleaning, is called for. Only plant in the middle of gaps where there is plenty of overhead light. In small gaps plant a group of three or four trees in a 1½ metre square— enrichment with just one tree provides no insurance against unforeseen loss. Plant healthy, sturdy trees and ensure good protection—see Chapter 4.

Any species suited to the site can be used, but if it is a strongly light-demanding species such as larch, pines, ash or oak make sure that subsequent thinning prevents these more recently established trees from being overtopped.

Thinning and pruning

Thinning out undesirable trees of poor form or unsuitable species can quickly change a woodland's condition. Frequently, a firewood merchant is willing to do this tidying job in exchange for the wood produced, though a check will need to be kept that only the poorer trees are taken.

Sometimes pruning side branches and singling forks of potentially good trees is sufficient to turn a wood into a reasonable crop. It is an

Plate 2.8 Gap in mixed broadleaved woodland large enough for enrichment by planting. If the wood is primarily for conservation, sporting or amenity, such openings and glades are greatly valued.

expensive operation but satisfying and can be done bit by bit when time permits.

Starting again

Sometimes a wood is so poor that there are simply not enough timber trees ever to make a crop; it really fits the expression 'useless scrub'. If the objective still remains that of producing timber the options are to clear and replant or to carry out intensive enrichment in swathes or enlarged gaps. Many areas of scrub are valuable wildlife resorts although they can degenerate into open land or, worse still, be cleared for development. Well-managed broadleaf plantations are just as valuable for wildlife as scruffy ones and provide a habitat which is more likely to survive long-term.

References for Further Reading

See Appendix 2.

Chapter 3

HEDGES AND HEDGEROW TREES

THE FIELD and farm boundary hedge has long been a feature of the British landscape, especially in the lowlands. While their rôle in demarcation and control of livestock has somewhat diminished, their importance for wildlife conservation and as an attractive feature has come to be appreciated (Plate 3.1). Less widely realised is the importance of hedgerow trees as timber: they are the source of one-fifth of all home-grown hardwood marketed in Britain. Proper care and

Plate 3.1 Attractive and characteristic scenery of small woodlands and hedgerow trees in Hampshire. They represent a major broadleaved tree resource.

maintenance of hedges and hedgerow trees builds an asset and adds immeasurably to the rural scene.

This chapter mainly concerns hedgerow trees but an appendix is included which summarises the principles of hedgerow management.

Hedgerow Timber

In Britain there are about ninety million trees in hedgerows, tiny clumps (less than 0.25 hectare) and lines such as avenues. The numbers and predominance of broadleaved species are shown in Table 3.1.

Hedgerow trees as a source of timber and other wood products have advantages and disadvantages. The open conditions encourage rapid radial growth and the trees reach large diameter sooner than their woodland counterparts. But this environment encourages heavy branching and development of a large crown. Compared with forest trees the proportion of crown wood to stem timber is greater and in large, old trees may add, in total yield of wood, as much again to what is in the trunk. There is plenty of firewood when a hedgerow tree is felled! As a very approximate indication Table 3.2 shows the amount of stem and branch wood for a given stem diameter.

Rapid growth, at least for broadleaved species, is no disadvantage and in the case of ash, beech and sycamore is a positive benefit resulting in better-quality, more uniform wood. Heavy side branching, however, unless controlled on the stem by pruning, results in large knots in the timber which greatly reduces its value. Another possible disadvantage is that hedgerow trees are prone to damage, mostly due to their boundary position and proximity to roads and tracks (see page 43), though such a position does allow good access for tending and harvesting.

Hedgerow Trees and the Farm

Like all plants, trees require light, moisture and nutrients for growth. As they grow and develop into large size the shade they cast and the moisture they take up may compete with the requirements of an adjacent crop. Shading effects mainly concern the north side of a tree and are only significant for broadleaves between mid-May and October when trees are in full leaf. Continuous shade is confined to near the tree well under the crown, and the degree of shade is dependent on tree species and height of crown break—the position where branching of the crown begins.

Dense shade is cast by beech, sycamore and conifers (except larches); relatively light shade is cast by larches, ash and cherry; oak shade is intermediate.

Table 3.1. Analysis of trees and tiny woods in Britain

	England	Wales	Scotland	Great Britain
		(millions of trees)		
Isolated trees				
Conifers	1.36	0.17	0.43	1.96
Broadleaves	12.99	1.91	1.25	16.15
% broadleaves	90.5	91.8	74.4	89.2
Trees in clumps				
Conifers	2.44	0.58	1.02	4.04
Broadleaves	21.02	3.28	4.31	28.61
% broadleaves	89.6	85.0	80.0	87.6
Linear features				
Conifers	1.45	0.70	1.19	3.34
Broadleaves	23.15	5.95	4.77	33.87
% broadleaves	94.1	89.5	80.0	91.0

Source: *Forestry Commission Census of Woodlands and Trees*, 1979–82.

Table 3.2. Estimate[1] of stem and branch wood weight[2] of broadleaved trees from stem diameter

Diameter of tree at breast height (DBH)[3] (cm)	Stem (tonnes)	Branch wood (tonnes)
25	0.4	0.12
30	0.6	0.20
40	1.2	0.55
50	1.9	1.0
60	2.6	1.5
70	3.3	2.5
80	4.2	3.7
100	6.0	6.0

Notes: 1. Figures are very approximate; differences in tree shape may cause up to 50 per cent variation from that shown.
2. Weight of wood in tonnes when tree is felled. The seasoned or air-dry weight in tonnes equals weight × 0.6 for most broadleaves and × 0.4 for poplars and willows.
3. Diameter at breast height (DBH) is measured on the stem at 1.3 m above ground (see Chapter 8).

Competition for moisture occurs in two ways. Trees transpire water like other plants, drawing on soil moisture reserves. Although rooting can be deep, even down to several metres, it is wrong to assume that moisture is only drawn from such levels. Much uptake occurs in the same rooting zone as crop plants, the top half metre or so of the soil. In addition, trees indirectly compete for moisture by intercepting rain before it reaches the ground. In summer a crown in full leaf can intercept all the rain falling during a light shower and the ground beneath will remain quite dry. Over a whole growing season this interception will typically reduce the amount of rain reaching ground level by ten to twenty per cent.

The combined effects of shade and water competition may reduce crop yields in the vicinity of a tree. But trees in a hedgerow will only affect crops on one or other sides and not all round. Moreover if they are on the northern side of a crop any shading effect will be minimal. In livestock management shade can be used to advantage in hot weather and during rain a tree's interception provides shelter for animals and humans alike to congregate to keep dry!

Trees are unlikely to compete for nutrients with other farm crops. Cereals and vegetables have much higher nutrient requirements than trees and these are generally satisfied directly by inputs of fertiliser. Indeed, heavy applications, particularly of nitrogen, can positively harm trees (see page 43).

There is little evidence that trees suppress other plants through mechanisms of allelopathy, production of toxic exudates from roots or leaves, or directly through leaf fall, though this used to be claimed for ash.

Establishment of Hedgerow Trees

The points below cover how best to include trees both when establishing a new hedge and when recruiting or adding trees to an existing hedge.

Location and spacing
From what has been said it is clear there are many benefits to be derived from hedgerow trees but, equally, it is sensible to minimise any adverse effects to other farm crops. Both location of hedgerow trees, their spacing and species (see below) are involved:

• Concentrate hedgerow trees along farm boundaries, beside roads and tracks, in field corners and at junctions of several fields.

• Beside roads and tracks establish trees on the southerly side so that their shade falls on sterile ground rather than a crop.

- Space trees at least twenty metres apart (Plate 3.2). Even when they are mature their crowns will hardly touch and thus will not form a line casting continuous shade. Between arable fields about thirty metres distance may be more appropriate, while at field corners or to create clumps much closer spacings can be used.

- Set the tree at least two metres back from the edge of a track or road, and avoid planting next to a telegraph pole, lamppost, etc.

- Protect the tree individually with a treeshelter (see Plate 4.7) and sturdy stake or other protection to mark its position clearly; subsequently treat as for other newly planted trees.

Plate 3.2 Eight-year-old beech saplings spaced at about 20 m apart beside temporary hedge of straw bales, Cumbria.

Species
Beech and evergreen conifers are best avoided as hedgerow trees. The once traditional choice in many parts of Britain, the elm, is no longer practicable owing to continuing high levels of Dutch Elm Disease, though many hedges still contain elm. Indeed, elm can be repeatedly trimmed as hedge with little risk of disease. If Dutch Elm Disease ever

loses virulence these 'hedge' elms can again be grown on to large size. Other undesirable species in certain situations are limes, because of the vigour and preponderance of basal shoots and the deposit of aphid 'honeydew', birches and poplars because of relatively short life, and special cultivars and 'garden' varieties which look out of place in the countryside.

Ash, oak, sycamore and wild cherry (gean) all make good hedgerow trees combining attractiveness with timber value. Field maple, alder and hornbeam are also satisfactory. The actual choice should, of course, take account of soil and site conditions as noted in Chapter 4.

Planting and recruiting
Planting hedgerow trees is no different from the techniques recommended in the next chapter if the trees are being planted at the same time as a new hedge. Where planting is filling a gap in an existing hedge it will be necessary either to use a larger plant, such as a 1.0 or 1.2 metre tall feathered whip, or ensure the gap width is equal to at least twice average hedge height and the tree planted in the middle. If very wide spacing between trees is planned plant two or even three close together in a group, say one metre apart, or rigorously replace any failures to ensure successful establishment at every point.

Recruiting trees from existing hedges is often a possibility. Although most hedges established today consist of only one or two species, and mainly of thorns with no potential for growing into trees, hedges dating back to the last century or earlier are frequently composed of many tree and shrub species. Regular clipping or laying will have kept the low hedge form but this treatment, however long carried on, never pre-cludes the tree species present from becoming normal trees once released from regular cutting back. To recruit hedgerow trees in this way simply place a clear marker protruding above the hedge at a point where there is a suitable species. When hedge trimming take care to leave the top uncut for about thirty centimetres either side of the marker. Vigorous growth will develop, usually consisting of several shoots and height will increase by half a metre or more in the following year. When next trimming the hedge one year or, more likely, two years later, leave the growth next to the marker uncut again and thin down the shoots to the best one or two stems. The marker can then be removed; the developing tree will be clearly visible with a thick stem.

One point to watch when recruiting trees from an old hedge is to make sure that the vigorous shoot being encouraged does not emerge from along or at the end of a previously laid stem. Laid stems of ash, especially, produce numerous shoots all of which have potential to grow

Plate 3.3 Numerous ash shoots vigorously growing up from recently laid stem. Select a shoot over the original root system to recruit as a hedgerow tree.

into trees. Select ones growing up from near the original base to avoid a weak 'S'-shaped stem (Plate 3.3).

Recruiting trees is cheap but requires care on the part of the tractor operator. As such trees begin to grow, the bottom two to three metres (the part which for many years was 'hedge') will be poorly formed. Eventually this will largely disappear though timber quality in this zone will always be very poor.

Another form of recruiting is to make use of naturally sown seedlings coming up in the protected environment of the hedge or as natural regeneration on adjacent bare mineral soil typical of many roadside embankments. Hedges, particularly of thorns and brambles, help protect any young tree seedlings within from browsing damage by rabbits, deer and livestock. It is not uncommon to see oak and sycamore in particular poking up through such hedges, while ash and birch are frequent colonisers of bare soil. Such trees will need identifying, marking, protecting and possibly release from overtopping to be recruited successfully as hedgerow timber.

Plate 3.4   New hedgerow trees, with livestock well excluded by strong fence, but (a) planted too close together, and (b) of unnecessarily large size requiring staking, and that rather untidily!

Protection and Maintenance

The requirements for hedgerow trees do not differ from other trees. The need for weed control will be small and localised, or non-existent, with no call for the undesirable practice of spraying a general herbicide along the hedge base. The trees must not be overtopped by the hedge and they must be protected from browsing (Plate 3.4); little else will be needed, apart possibly from pruning.

Pruning

In general, pruning forest trees is little practised but an exception should be made for hedgerow trees. As mentioned, hedgerow trees will develop heavy branches and these must be cut off on the lower bole (trunk), say to four or five metres, if a reasonable butt of timber is to be grown. Such pruning should be carried out before branches become more than about five centimetres thick and usually in two stages: to about two metres up the stem when the tree is about five metres tall and, if desired, to four or five metres when it is eight to ten metres tall.

Such attention to pruning has a second rôle. Side branches from trees growing next to a road or track, if uncontrolled, become a hazard constricting access along a track or illegally obstructing a public highway. Pruning side branches early in the life of a tree in the way suggested, will completely avoid this problem and make the tree relatively safe and, indeed, almost unclimbable too!

One other pruning operation which may be necessary, especially for recruited trees, is singling of forks to one stem. A single stem to at least six metres is desirable and pruning away any second leaders should be done once the tree has emerged above hedge height.

Felling

Procedures do not differ from those for forest trees though care and warnings are necessary next to public highways and other rights of way.

Problems with Hedgerow Trees

Barking by livestock

Horses, sheep, cattle, pigs and goats will all strip bark from trees during cold weather in winter and early spring. No tree species is immune from this problem and if stripping ring-barks the stem the tree will die. Stripping is worst when land is overstocked or there is insufficient feed; proper care of livestock is much better than erecting expensive individual fences around trees at risk.

Incorporating trees into a fence

All too often a conveniently placed tree is used as a fence post with wire attached and nails hammered in. Such metal will in time become ingrown and ultimately occluded with no visible sign. When felled and sawn such bits of metal are a great hazard, severely damaging saws and, occasionally, the operator. Use of trees as substitutes for posts should be avoided if at all possible.

Machine damage

Next to cultivated fields, roads and tracks, trees are more at risk from damage by moving vehicles. Commonly, this involves loss of bark at the base which is not only unsightly but is a potential entry site for fungal infection.

Trees and cereal cultivation

There is some evidence that two practices in arable cropping, intensive ploughing of surface soil and heavy applications of nitrogenous fertilisers,

Plate 3.5   Making room for wires—the oak is probably about sixty years of age.

are harmful to trees. Ploughing adjacent to trees severs surface roots and high applications of nitrogen may cause root scorching. Ash, which tends to be shallow rooting, seems especially at risk and these factors are believed to contribute to what is labelled 'ash decline', a condition where mature trees show progressive dieback of the crown. The recent increase in ash decline and dieback of individual trees on farmland appears to reflect changing farming practices in modern times, particularly the conversion from pasture to arable cropping.

Safety

The question of trees next to highways and the hazard they represent to passing traffic has been mentioned. Appropriate precautions are planting at least two metres back from the road edge and pruning side branches. Additional hazards are interference with overhead wires and lines (Plate 3.5) and falling branches in gales or after heavy snowfall. Such problems should be foreseen by inspecting trees from time to time, perhaps every other year, when they are in leaf. Branches which are likely to cause interference or are suspect, such as those diseased or prematurely withered, can then be identified for removal by pruning.

Managing Farm Hedges

Notes by Mr M. Hellewell, reproduced by kind permission of ADAS.

Hedges are valuable features that need regular and careful maintenance according to a long-term plan.

Trimming

This stimulates growth of side shoots, making the hedge denser and stock-proof.

- Do not trim every year. Hedging plants only flower on shoots at least one year old—so, to encourage flowers and berries, trim only every two or three years; or trim only one side each year. This reduces maintenance costs.

- Trim in late winter, but avoid periods of hard frost—this ensures that birds and small mammals have a chance to eat the berries, and does not disturb nesting birds.

- Leave the hedge at least 1.4 m high and preferably 1.8 m high.

- Allow some established saplings to grow on—preferably not elms, which are probably infected with elm disease. Tag selected saplings every 50 m or so as a reminder.

There is no 'right' shape for a hedge. Trimming to an 'A' shape has advantages in that it is economical to trim and allows the hedgerow saplings to grow up to provide song posts for small birds.

However, when the hedge is on a bank, or there is rich and attractive ground flora along the edge, a narrow, vertically sided hedge is better. This sort of ground vegetation is itself valuable for wildlife, and banks provide safer resting sites for ground-nesting birds such as partridges. The 'A'-shaped hedge, with its wide base, can suppress this vegetation and destroy the resting sites.

Hedge Laying

Eventually hedges will start becoming thin and 'gappy' at the base. They should then be left untrimmed for a few years until ready for laying, which rejuvenates the hedge and makes it stock-proof once more.

- For laying, the main stems should be 3.0–3.5 m high and about 50–100 mm thick at the base.

- Lay hedges on a 15–20 year rotation. This ensures that there are hedges at all stages of growth over the farm.

- The best time for laying hedges is from mid-November until early March.

- Leave hedges untrimmed for one or two years after laying to give time for new shoots to start growing.

Coppicing

If the hedge is too gappy or the stems of the hedge are too thick for laying, then coppicing the hedge is the best way to rejuvenate it. An experienced hedger can judge when a neglected hedge is no longer suitable for laying. For coppicing:

- Cut all the hedge plants down to a height of 75 mm above ground level, and leave to grow up once more.

- Do not cut the hedge down to 1.0–1.5 m high because the stems will then grown 'bushy' heads and the base of the hedge will remain thin.

- If the hedge is not needed as a livestock barrier, coppicing on an 8–12 year rotation is an economic method of hedge management.

Gapping

This is likely to be necessary where management has been neglected, but gaps will appear even in well-managed hedges. Gaps under trees should be closed using post-and-rail fencing. All other gaps should be replanted, preferably in October or November after cleaning and digging the soil over. For the transplants:

- Use even-sized 2 year old transplants (which will be three to four years old) 450–600 mm in height.

- If possible, use plants raised on poorer soil than that in the hedge line.

- Hawthorn, blackthorn, hazel and field maple are common suitable species. Try to obtain these from local sources.

- Plant the seedlings in staggered rows, 250 mm apart; protect from stock and rabbits with wire fencing and keep weeded and watered until established.

Grant Aid

CAP grants for planting, re-planting and hedge improvement (e.g. hedge laying) are available under the Farm and Conservation Grant Scheme at the rate of 40 per cent outside LFAs and 50 per cent within them. For further information and advice contact your nearest Agricultural Adviser.

Chapter 4

STARTING WITH BARE GROUND

WITH MUCH talk about alternative uses for land 'coming out of agriculture', a variety of attractive grants for tree planting and growing energy in the form of fuelwood, afforesting bare ground is an increasingly important skill to master. The subject of tree planting on the farm resolves into four questions: for what purpose, where, which species, and how? The first of these, the purpose or object of planting, has been covered in Chapter 1 and will only be referred to again where it directly affects practices.

In passing it is worth noting that trees are rarely established by sowing the ground where the crop is to grow, as with cereals and most vegetables, but by planting young trees, usually one to three years old, raised in special nurseries. This distinction is emphasised since it influences all stages of establishment.

WHERE TO PLANT

Both the object of planting and ground conditions play a part in the decision of where to plant. Four different kinds of planting are considered.

Shelterbelts, Blocks and Windbreaks

The location of woodland blocks or narrow belts of trees to provide shelter is of considerable importance in determining their effectiveness. The first point to consider is what is being sheltered. Both belts and blocks are suitable for sheltering stock, the advantage of the latter being that the animals can move into the lee of the block irrespective of wind direction. Shelterbelts, on the other hand, provide a wider zone of reduced wind speeds when the wind is blowing at right-angles to their long axes and are more suitable for sheltering immobile crops or buildings.

The second consideration is topographic position. Poorly drained sites and frost hollows should be avoided to promote stability and reasonable growth rates, and to minimise poaching of land adjacent to the trees by concentrations of animals. Blocks and belts should be located to enhance the shelter effect of natural land forms, such as the windward side and summit of a ridge or spur. Shelterbelts should be oriented at right-angles to the prevailing wind direction, of sufficient length and located at regular intervals to maximise their effect. (See Chapter 5 for details.) Thought should be given to the long-term effects on adjacent land of shading and, possibly, debris. For example, avoid planting on the south side of buildings, or too close, and avoid heavy shade on tracks and roads which can lead to slow drying and icy conditions in winter.

Thirdly, shape and size should be considered. Fencing is a major element of establishment costs and rectangular blocks will have lower fencing costs per unit area than long thin strips or belts. A block of about ten hectares will also have potential for economic timber production which is not normally the case in narrow shelterbelts, and a 'Manx leg' or L-shaped design can increase the value of a block by providing shelter from a number of wind directions. On the other hand, larger blocks take up more land than narrow shelterbelts and for this reason are normally preferred on poorer grades of land.

Woodlands for Timber, Firewood and other Forest Produce

Although shelterbelts will provide some forest products, woodlands planted specifically for this purpose are not severely constrained by location. Indeed, provided access is reasonable, planting can be done anywhere though rate of tree growth achieved will, of course, vary with site. The following points should be borne in mind when locating sites for new planting.

1. Most farms can easily accommodate 5–10 per cent of land under trees without seriously prejudicing crop yields while adding to overall prosperity, and on some land total farm yield increases with woodland shelter occupying up to 25 per cent of the farm.

2. To minimise competition with farm crops, plant waste land or those parts of low agricultural potential such as steep slopes, rocky areas, wet or poorly drained ground, awkward areas and field corners where, perhaps, one short fence can enclose the site (Plate 4.1). There is also a place for line plantings beside tracks, roads, water-

Plate 4.1   Single fence across corner of field effectively enclosing a triangle of ground and planted with sixty trees.

courses and in the proximity of buildings, but mainly for amenity purposes.

3. Where the intention is to plant land, perhaps formerly under productive arable or pasture, to grow biomass on short rotations for fuel production, the method of harvesting will largely dictate the optimum site. Although still experimental, growing woody biomass using poplars, willows or exotic species such as southern beech or hardy eucalypts on one- to five-year rotations for fuelwood, or up to ten years for wood chips, does have promise and is quite common in Europe (Plate 4.2). To work efficiently, the site must be even with a slope of less than five degrees especially if tractor access for machine harvesting of the shoots is planned.

4. Generally, to minimise fencing requirements and costs of tending operations and thinning, compact blocks of woodland are preferable to long strips. Of course, with small plantings of only a few hundred trees and where tree shelters or other individual protection is used compactness is a less important cost factor (Plate 4.3). The overriding influence of woodland size and costs of establishment, particularly

Plate 4.2   Somerset farmer Hugh Male standing beside a two-
year-old willow coppice crop being grown for biomass.

fence length per hectare enclosed, accounts for the differential rates
of grants according to area of planting, regeneration, etc., provided
through the Forestry Commission.

Amenity and Conservation Plantings

With relatively little of Britain under forest and woodland almost any
tree planting adds to the amenity and to conservation interest (in a
general sense) in a locality. Clearly, trees planted purely for pleasure
will be of a species the owner likes but it remains an essential maxim that
it is only worth planting what has a reasonably assured chance of
success. Failure or very slow growth is disappointing.

Plate 4.3 Narrow strip of new planting with trees in individual tree shelters. Fencing would have been prohibitively expensive though use of brown-tinted tree shelters would have made them much less obtrusive.

Much can be said, and has been written on this subject, but a few observations are worth noting.

- Avoid fussy planting of many species, which looks bitty. Concentrate on establishing groups of trees of one or two species.

- Planting large trees, called standards or half-standards in the trade, for instant effect is rarely worth while. They take a long time to establish, need robust stakes and cost many times more than transplants. A well-planted transplant, 50 centimetres tall and properly weeded and protected, will in five years often have caught up the larger tree, be healthier and have cost less than half the total outlay.

- To encourage conservation, plant species native to the locality and, of course, avoid planting right up to existing features of interest such as streams, ponds, marshy ground and archaeological remains—dykes, mounds, etc.

Game Coverts and Copses

Carefully located cover can greatly enhance the sporting potential of open land whether for game, foxes or rough shooting. The area devoted to such cover does not need to be large; allocating ten per cent of a farm will generally provide enough for this purpose. Indeed, in many instances improving sporting potential, and indirectly a farm's amenity and wildlife value as well, will mainly be a question of making the most of existing woods. If necessary, glades and warm sunlit rides can be provided, and berried plants and shrubs encouraged. Shelter and draughtiness should be checked and the wood could even be restructured to give flushing cover—small areas of low vegetation near, but not at, the edge will encourage pheasant flight slanting upwards.

Adding sporting cover to a farm by planting or allowing natural scrub to develop should not be haphazard. The lie of the land, exposure, access, animal species to be encouraged all need to be considered and specialist advice should be sought if a major investment is planned in improving a farm's or estate's sporting. The Game Conservancy at Fordingbridge provides this service.

WHAT SPECIES?

Trees and woodlands grow for a long time. The decision of what to plant is therefore immensely important—there is no end-of-year harvest and opportunity for change. For woodlands managed for larger-size timber the decision of what species to plant is a once-in-a-lifetime opportunity. This commitment might seem an almost intolerable burden but complete failure is rare and there is much pleasure in posterity where a healthy stand can be enjoyed for many years. Impressive woodland, healthy, well grown and well tended, speaks of the skill of former generations. The opportunity to add one's own mark remains just the same, or is indeed enhanced in the 1990s, as Britain continues to rebuild its forest estate from the all-time low of only five per cent of land wooded at the turn of the century.

Deciding what to plant has two main aspects. Many species are not interchangeable, one simply cannot be swopped for the other and the same result be achieved. Therefore, knowing the purpose the trees are intended for—timber, fuelwood, shelterbelt, wildlife enhancement—affects the choice because each species has a different blend of attributes to bring. And, if there are several different aims for the new woodland, examining these species' characteristics allows the right one or right combination of several to be planted. The principal characteristics of important tree species suitable for Britain are listed in Appendix 1 and some basic considerations are shown in Table 4.1.

The second aspect of species choice is knowing what will grow well on the site in question. Britain has a long history of species' trials, and recommendations for species' choice by site types can be made with reasonable confidence—Appendix 1 lists suitable conditions by species. A general point can, however, be made. The better the site (the less exposed and the more fertile it is), the wider the choice of species that will grow well. The reason why most afforestation in the uplands is with spruces and pines, and mostly only one species of each, is because few broadleaves will grow well in the exposed conditions on poor acid soils.

Table 4.2 recommends species to consider by broad site types. It is very generalised, and features of the local site should also be considered, particularly whether it is unusually frost-prone, beside a stream or river, or very poorly drained.

In addition to considerations of purpose and site other factors which can influence the final choice include finance, and the need for an early return from investment; preference for native species where wildlife

Table 4.1. Preliminary considerations for species choice

Purpose	Desirable features	Examples
Timber and other high-quality uses	Straight stems, fine branches, sound and marketable wood known to trade.	Most conifers but only principal broadleaves—oak, beech, ash, sycamore, cherry, sweet chestnut, etc.
Fuelwood	Rapid initial growth coppice ability	Broadleaves
Pulpwood	Rapid growth, straight stems	Conifers and any straight-stemmed broadleaves
Shelter	Tolerate exposure persistent branching	Many conifers, sycamore, beech
Conservation	Native species, especially to locality	see Appendix 1
Amenity	Visual characteristics Longevity	see Appendix 1

Table 4.2. Commoner species suited to the main site types in Britain

Soil	Lowland		Upland	
	dry	*moist*	*sheltered*	*exposed*
fertile, brown earth, pH 5–7	pine, larch most broadleaves	Douglas fir most conifers and broadleaves	Douglas fir spruces, sycamore, beech	(rare)
acid, pH less than 5				
sandy	pine, sweet chestnut, birch		pine, larch	pine, birches
clayey	oak, hornbeam alder	Norway spruce oak	spruces	Sitka spruce lodgepole pine rowan, alders
alkaline, pH greater than 7	Corsican pine ash, sycamore cherry, beech	Norway spruce ash, sycamore cherry, beech	ash, sycamore Norway spruce beech	(rare)

conservation is uppermost; actual availability of plants; and the risk of disease (as for elm planting at the present time).

The practice of using a conifer nurse was referred to in Chapter 2 (page 23). Where the aim is eventually to establish a broadleaved stand, groups of final crop trees (commonly about 25 per cent of the total) can be planted within a matrix of conifers—or other fast growing, shorter-lived broadleaves. The nurse species encourages good stem form in the final crop trees and provides an early return of useful produce from thinnings, such as larch fencing posts. (The value of conifers in this respect is less important now that there is a better market for small hardwood thinnings.) Care is needed to ensure that the nurse does not swamp the desired long-term crop (see page 20): nurse trees should be removed preferentially in thinnings and after perhaps 35 years will have largely disappeared.

The choice of species is crucial, but the performance of the chosen species can also be affected by the location from which its seed was collected. Some localities produce stands whose genetic make-up is distinctive and regularly reproducible; these are called provenances. For many introduced conifers there are important provenance differences affecting such things as frost tolerance, rate of growth, form and habit of the tree. Nurseries will generally know the source of the seed they use, and it is reasonably safe to assume that the provenance of trees purchased for planting from reputable nurseries is suitable for anywhere in Britain. So far as native species are concerned substantial provenance differences have not been confirmed.

All oak and beech raised for planting woodlands should, under European Community guidelines, have come from seed from registered stands. Use of poplar and willow is also controlled, owing to the incidence of disease, and only certain clones can legally be supplied. Seed sources of most of the important species of conifers are controlled under EC regulations for forest reproductive material, and only these are generally available from nurseries. In general try to use local provenances of the common species and ask the nurseryman to specify the source of his seed.

How to Plant

Ground Preparation

The object of ground preparation is to give the tree the best possible start—to ensure it survives and grows. Reasonably robust plants are used, so the degree of cultivation need not match that required to nurture a field of corn from seed. Indeed, the amount of preparation of the ground before planting can vary from nil for replanting recently cleared woodland sites (Plate 4.4) to the installation of open field drains and deep-furrow cultivation on wet, poorly drained, inhospitable sites.

The drainage of sites prior to planting is expensive. On the scale of planting contemplated by most farmers it is probably better either not to plant an excessively wet site or to use tolerant species such as alder, willows, poplar or lodgepole pine. They should be planted on the fringe of the wet area or where natural humps or rocks provide some locally better drainage.

Cultivation of lowland and upland sites
For most lowland sites soil cultivation is confined to the digging associated with the planting operation itself. On upland sites spaced furrow ploughing, which turns over a ribbon of turf, provides an elevated and better drained planting position and gives weed suppression for one or even two years. It is also easier to plant into, particularly on the heavier peaty-gleys. Spaced ploughing should only be considered if the equipment is easily to hand and more than two hectares are being planted. On very exposed sites such ploughing can increase the instability of trees in later life as rooting direction is constrained. In such situations either carry out complete ploughing (leaving no ribbons of turf and adjacent furrows), or dig individual turves.

Plate 4.4   Site ready for planting. The recently felled previous crop has been extracted and lop and top stacked and burned.

Early indications of Forestry Commission trials on ADAS experimental husbandry farms suggest that ploughing before planting merely worsens the weed problems on both old pasture and ex-arable land. Direct planting with localised weed control appears preferable.

Pre-planting weed control
Weeds are a major competitor to trees and at every stage of establishment the grower of woodland should seek to minimise their harmful influence. Where the 'bare' site is covered in bracken, dense grass swards or herbaceous or low woody growth a pre-planting herbicide application helps bring the weed problem under control from the outset. There are many suitable herbicides including glyphosate, atrazine/dalapon and propyzamide, but the aim should be to use one which kills the weeds and does not merely desiccate the foliage or arrest growth.

Forestry Commission Field Book 8 *The Use of Herbicides in the Forest* and the instructions which accompany every herbicide provide sufficient information for carrying out effective weed control in a legal and safe way.

The reduction of weed growth before planting by swiping, mowing or simply burning off achieves little or no weed control, although such operations may be appropriate to make planting easier; the use of livestock to clear an area for planting should not be forgotten.

Season of Planting

Planting is winter work which can be carried out at any time the ground is not frozen or snow-covered. The best months are November, December, late February, March and early April. Plants should still be dormant when put in and a cool, moist day with rain forecast provides the ideal conditions.

Planting in late spring and summer is feasible with great care but unless trees can be given the care they would have in the garden—weekly watering, careful weed control—losses will usually be unacceptably high.

Laying out Planting Positions

In general, trees are planted at about two-metre spacing (2,500 per hectare) but up to three-metre spacing (1,100 per hectare) for some broadleaves in the lowlands. The actual number is a compromise between cost—which increases with number per hectare—and ensuring the ground is adequately stocked. Adequate stocking is needed to suppress weeds, create conditions of mutual shelter and competition (as in forest stands), and provide enough trees from which a reasonable final crop can be selected.

Trees are generally planted in straight lines or rows (it is hard to contrive a genuinely random or 'natural' distribution) for ease of management and to ensure even stocking over the site. Rows should terminate at a ride or track and not run up and down hillsides if two or more species are planted in strips.

Method of Planting

The simplest way to plant a small tree is to dig a slit or notch in the ground, carefully insert the roots, spread them, and close the slit by firming the soil with the heel of the foot on either side. Several hundred trees per day can be planted by this method. This is the minimum of cultivation and will be adequate on all but the heaviest clays where slits or notches tend to open when the soil dries. A more time-consuming method is to plant in pits; a pit about 30 × 30 × 30 cm is dug, the tree placed in the centre and the soil firmed around the roots. Such care may lead to some initial improvement in growth but at most only about two hundred trees per day can be planted.

'Screef' planting involves removing the surface vegetation from a small area around each tree prior to planting, in order to reduce root competition. For short, dense grass it is usually better to use spot weed control with a pre-planting herbicide, especially on dry sites where the soil is liable to crack.

Whatever method is chosen, make sure the tree is inserted into the soil only as far as the root collar—the junction between shoot and root—and that the roots are spread out rather than being in a tight bunch. Also make sure that the tree is planted vertically and not at an angle. Plant only living trees (!) and rigorously reject (cull) any obviously damaged or weakly ones.

Obtaining Plants

There are many nurseries supplying young trees. Place an order as far in advance of the intended planting date as possible. As soon as the plants are delivered their quality and well-being should be examined. If the plants are damaged, their roots are at all dry or their stems brown under the bark they should be rejected. (Live plants are green under the bark—check by making a nick with the thumbnail on a small sample.)

If the plants are in polythene bags they can be stored for up to about a month in a cool frost-free place out of the sun without suffering too much harm. Plants can be temporarily stored on site by heeling them in—they are placed in a trench and soil firmed up against the roots to keep them moist.

When planting, continue to protect the plants from direct sunlight and ensure that their roots never dry out, even for a few minutes. Avoid throwing bags of plants around or handling them roughly in any way.

Plant type

The customary and cheapest plants to use are bare-rooted seedlings and transplants. The latter are seedlings which have been moved from one bed to another in the nursery between their first and second years; in the trade this is known as 1 + 1. Most important, however, is the size of the plants. They should be sturdy, with shoots 30–60 cm tall, have a thick root collar (more than 5 mm) and be well furnished with roots. Do not bother to plant tall spindly trees or ones with poorly developed roots. The nurseryman generally supplies about 10 per cent more plants than ordered to permit this additional culling.

Larger plants such as feathered whips (1–1.5 m tall, well furnished with branches), half-standards and standards are rarely worth the extra expense. Trees in containers, more expensive than bare-rooted ones of the same size, confer no growth advantage and may tempt the buyer to plant in late spring or summer, which is undesirable; they are really for garden work.

Fertilising

On all lowland sites fertilising at planting will probably be unnecessary, though a small addition of phosphate to conifers in the Weald and on southern heaths may be beneficial. In general, good weed control is much more important. In the uplands phosphate should be added for conifers planted on peats, peaty gleys and poorer surface-water gleys. Apply 100 grammes of rock phosphate per plant, or half this amount of 'triple super phosphate'.

WEED CONTROL

Why Control Weeds?

The importance of good weed control has already been stressed. Rank weed growth competes with newly planted trees for moisture, nutrients and, if overtopping the trees, light. Weeds can also harbour animals such as mice and voles which gnaw bark, and can smother small trees following snowfall. In the spring, dead grass, heather and gorse are an acute fire hazard. It is sometimes claimed that weeds confer some shelter to young trees on exposed sites. This has been hard to prove although it seems appealing; however, the benefits of not having weed competition in the vicinity of a tree are almost certainly much more important.

Which kind of weed damage is most important varies with site and species. In the uplands dense grass swards are a serious fire hazard and heather directly suppresses the growth of spruces by interfering with root mycorrhizal relationships and upsetting nutrient uptake. Spruce planted in heather can stagnate in a state of check for years, hardly growing at all, if the heather is left uncontrolled. In the lowlands, moisture competition at the start of the growing season, in May and June, is the most stressful effect of weed competition, particularly for broadleaves. Good weed control (weeds being killed, not just cut, especially on grassy sites) can lead to better survival and tripling of the early height growth of many species. Indeed, the typical mown grass environment seen in so many parks and grounds is amongst the worst and most competitive environments for a tree.

How to Control Weeds

Cutting methods

In the past most weed control involved cutting back weeds with a sickle or hook and had to be carried out several times a year on some sites to ensure trees survived. Control of weed growth was temporary and at each weeding the young trees were at risk themselves from inadvertent cutting! With wide spacings mechanical weeding with tractor-mounted flails and rotating cutters is feasible between rows, though weeds still remain near and in line with the trees. The main drawback of cutting is that weeds are not killed and it is the least desirable method except, perhaps, where conservation is important. Even for conservation, regular cutting tends to promote grasses at the expense of herbaceous vegetation. Grass killing herbicides might be positively beneficial.

Killing weeds by herbicide
Killing weeds with herbicide is generally the cheapest and most effective control. Herbicides kill outright or severely check weeds and therefore eliminate their competition for a time. Many herbicides exist, and almost any weed type can be controlled. Care is needed when treating broadleaved crops since herbicides lethal to herbaceous weeds will also kill the trees. It will be necessary to use a tree guard with the applicator or grow the trees in tree shelters (see below).

Mulching
Mulching is an effective control method if it is dense enough to suppress weeds or prevent them from growing altogether. Thick polythene sheeting, old fertiliser bags (washed of residual fertiliser), bituminous felt, a layer of bark or old carpet are all suitable and may be worth considering for small plantings of twenty or thirty trees.

Period and Extent of Weed Control

Weeding should be done when it is needed! Whatever method is used, the aim is to create a weed-free zone around each tree. In the lowlands weeding should be carried out each year until trees are at least 2 metres tall, i.e. for three to six years after planting, and in the uplands until trees have grown above competing vegetation. During the year weed early in the growing season to be effective; certainly for the lowlands most benefit is obtained when there is good weed control in the May to July period of rapid growth. The time of application of herbicide will, of course, depend on the formulation and manufacturer's recommendations—for example, effective bracken-control herbicides must be applied in late June/July, whereas some soil-acting herbicides, e.g. propyzamide, are only applied in early winter.

Weeds should be controlled at least to a radius of 60 centimetres around the tree or in a swathe along the row of one metre wide.

CLEANING AND BRASHING

Cleaning is a form of weed control necessary in some plantations in the thicket to small-pole stage, several years before first thinning, where unwanted woody growth or climbers are interfering with the crop and need cutting out (Plate 4.5). It is a slow job but often essential on former woodland sites and in plantations on calcareous soils where climbers

Plate 4.5   Mechanical cleaning between rows of nine-year-old oak to cut out birch, gorse and other competing woody growth.

such as clematis and honeysuckle can overwhelm a crop if they are uncontrolled. Unwanted woody growth might include hazel, birch, sallows, elder, broom and gorse and coppice shoots coming up from stumps of a previous crop.

Brashing is low pruning up the stem to 1.8 m to provide access for inspection and shooting. It is not essential to carry out complete brashing—25 per cent is adequate for inspection, for example—and the brashing of shelterbelts will decrease their effectiveness.

PROTECTION

Trees may require protection from animal damage, fire, climatic extremes, pests and diseases.

Mammal Damage

Newly established crops

Young trees are susceptible to the browsing, gnawing of bark and trampling caused by many different animals but most importantly livestock, voles and mice, rabbits and deer. For small plantings (less than about 1 hectare) individual tree protection using tree shelters will be adequate (Plate 4.6). A tree shelter is a plastic tube, usually 1.2 metres tall, inside which the tree grows. It is secured to the ground by a stake and is left around the tree until it breaks down after six or seven years by which time the trees will be well out of the top and above browse height. If fallow or red deer are present taller tree shelters up to 2.0 metres will be needed. If tree planting is in fields grazed by cows, tree shelters secured with two stakes and wrapped around with barbed wire have proved effective; special fences are very costly and should be used on only a few trees (Plate 4.7). Normally in such field planting it will be better to fence off a corner or strip and protect in the normal way—see Plates 3.4 and 4.1.

Tree shelters also enhance early growth, make weed control with herbicide safer and easier, and permit rapid identification of the planting spot for inspection of trees. They also increase the tree's chance of survival in hot, dry years.

For larger areas of planting (more than 2 hectares) individual tree protection becomes too expensive and conventional fencing, to a standard to exclude the harmful animal, is cheaper.

Older crops

As well as fencing, or individual tree protection, supplementary control of rabbit populations through rough shooting or winter gassing will be of benefit to arable crops and woodland alike. Even mature trees of beech and sycamore are at risk from basal bark stripping by rabbits in cold winters when snow lies. In large forests deer management is an integral part of damage control.

The other seriously damaging animal of older stands is the grey squirrel. Oak, beech, sycamore and maple are worst affected but all species, including conifers, may be badly damaged or killed. Bark-stripping damage, which frequently ring-barks the tree in the crown,

Plate 4.6 Tree shelter, 1.2 m tall, providing complete protection from mammal damage and easy weeding with herbicide for newly planted tree—in this instance a wild cherry (leaves can be seen inside).

Plate 4.7 Robust and costly protection for tree planted in a field. This scale of protection is necessary, though there are cheaper alternatives than illustrated, where cows and horses graze; tree planting may be better at the field edge such as illustrated in Plate 3.4.

Plate 4.8 Bark stripping of hawthorn. This damage results from overstocking and can affect all tree species; it occurs mainly in winter and can be caused by cattle, horses and pigs as well as sheep.

mostly occurs between May and July in young pole stage crops when trees are 8–15 metres tall. Damage does not occur every year but can be sufficiently devastating to make regular control by trapping, poison-baiting, and shooting an essential part of management of such broad-leaved crops.

Livestock can damage woodlands of any age if stocking rates are too high or animals are left in the wood for too long (Plate 4.8). Woodlands can be a useful farm asset providing shelter in severe weather but their use by livestock must be carefully regulated.

Fire

The main threat from fire is in newly established plantations with rank growth of grass, heather or gorse and broom. The risk is highest in the spring before new growth has emerged and the previous year's dead vegetation becomes tinder-dry in a desiccating March wind!

For small plantings specific fire precautions will be unnecessary, especially if the whole wood is contained within the farm and not adjacent to a public place and if good weed control is practised.

Climatic Extremes

Drought
Forest trees are not irrigated, though obviously if there are only a few newly planted trees giving each a bucketful of water during a pro-longed dry spell in the summer will help survival. The best insurance against 'drought' death after planting is attention to careful handling in the first place and a high standard of weed control to eliminate the main source of competition for soil moisture.

Winter cold and frost
Tree species vary greatly in their hardiness to winter cold and unseasonable frosts. All native species are hardy in British winters but exotics such as southern beech, eucalypts and Monterey cypress may be damaged if temperatures fall below minus 15 degrees centigrade. Such species are probably best avoided except in milder westerly localities.

Late spring and early autumn frosts are a more serious and intractable hazard. Once the young leaves have emerged (flushing) all species are susceptible, but some more so than others. Walnut, ash, oak and spruces are generally susceptible to late frosts while hornbeam, wild cherry, larches and pines are much less so. If the planting site is a well-known frost hollow, typically low-lying ground near water where cold night air accumulates, avoid the more susceptible species. Also good weed control is again a help since colder air and lower temperatures are found over thick grass swards on frosty nights than over bare soil. Where planting is being carried out on an older woodland site the retention of twenty or thirty trees per hectare, giving a dappled shade effect, greatly reduces the incidence of frost damage and can allow the establishment of more sensitive species.

Trees are rarely killed by frost but can be repeatedly damaged every year—frost pruned—leading to poor growth, forked and deformed stems. If this happens with broadleaves one possible solution is to cut back the tree to ground level, an operation called stumping back. In the following year a tall shoot rapidly grows which will often elevate the leader above the very coldest zone 20–60 centimetres above ground. Once trees are over two metres high frost becomes less of a problem.

Wind

Wind is mainly a hazard of old trees with decay in roots or branches and pole-stage crops established on wet, poorly rootable soils where trees can prematurely blow over. The inspection of old trees, especially if they are beside public highways, can sometimes reveal signs of internal decay or weakness. Look for fungal brackets or toadstools, patches of dead bark, weeping or bleeding from bark, or crown dieback; if there is reason for concern, seek advice. The problems of windthrow of whole crops or shelterbelts is unlikely in woodlands of farm scale except in storms of 1987 magnitude.

Wind may also be a hazard for young trees in the few years after planting, especially on moist and clay soils. Large plants swaying in the wind may develop 'sockets' in the soil, which fill with water and cause further trouble; Douglas fir, for instance, is prone to this trouble. The farmer should avoid over-large plants. Loosened and socketed plants should be firmed, especially in the spring and in extreme cases may have to be given temporary support.

Pests and Diseases

Trees suffer from pests and diseases like other plants. The main way to prevent this is by avoiding susceptible species: for example, elm should not be planted and if poplars and willows are chosen, only canker-resistant clones should be used. Secondly, pursue good silviculture to maintain good vigour. Slow-growing trees, for whatever reason, are generally more at risk from pests and diseases. The regular control of pests and diseases by spraying with insecticide or fungicide is not practised in forestry with the exception that conifer stumps are treated with urea immediately after cutting. This is to prevent infection from *Fomes annosus* which can rot wood saprophytically and kill adjacent living trees in root contact parasitically. This treatment is especially important for pines on calcareous soils.

If there are signs of many trees in a crop, say more than one in ten or patches of four or more, being attacked or showing damage symptoms advice should be sought from a Forestry Commission Private Woodlands Officer. Signs to look for are defoliation, dieback, small or deformed leaves, bud death or leader loss, holes in bark, weeping of fluid and dead bark.

References for Further Reading

See Appendix 2.

Chapter 5

THE INFLUENCES OF WOODLAND ON THE FARM

'WHEN FARM-LANDS are exposed to high winds, interspersing them with strips or masses of plantation is attended with obviously important advantages,' wrote Walter Nicol in *The Planter's Kalendar* in 1812. 'Not only are such lands rendered more congenial to the growth of grass, and corn, and the health of pasturing animals, but the local climate is improved.'

The influence of woodland and trees on the farm extends far beyond the provision of wood. Some of the effects are regarded as beneficial, such as shelter, the screening of buildings, the creation of habitats for shooting and wildlife, and the maintenance of landscapes, while others, such as the harbouring of pests, are held to be harmful. All these and more have importance in different parts of the country and for different types of farming.

Close attention at the design stage to the real objectives of planting is essential, since trees are intended to live for a long time and mistakes are difficult to correct. It is better to design the planting so that it achieves specified objectives really well rather than attempting to satisfy several basically conflicting aims and serving none properly.

PHYSICAL EFFECTS OF WOODLAND

Shelterbelts

The main objective of a shelterbelt is to give protection to vegetation, livestock or buildings from the harmful effects of wind. Shelter may be particularly helpful in orchards, for young stock, for intensively managed grazings and, in parts of the country where dry winds often blow in spring over newly sown and rolled fields, as a means of controlling soil erosion.

What shelterbelts do

Wind currents flow more or less parallel to the land surface and increase in velocity with height above the ground. The effect of a shelterbelt is to lift these wind currents, preferably without causing violent eddies and disturbance. A cushion of air develops in front of the belt, deflecting the main windstream up its slope. Some air passes through the cushion and through the belt itself, which should act as a filter rather than a barrier; the filtered air should then emerge from the leeward edge of the belt at a reduced velocity and should act as a slow-moving cushion of rolling eddies, preventing the main airstream, which has passed over the top of the belt, from returning to the ground until it is a considerable distance downwind. (See Figure 5.1.)

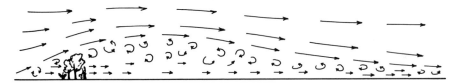

Figure 5.1   Pattern of wind flow over and through a narrow permeable shelterbelt: small rolling eddies creating a long zone of shelter.

There is a close connection between the height of a shelterbelt and the distance over which a reduction of wind speed is provided. Consequently it is usual to express distances, both upwind and downwind of a shelterbelt, in terms of the height of the main trees. The effect of a shelterbelt in reducing the wind speed near the ground (say at 1 to 1½ metres from the ground) may be detected for about nine times its height upwind and about thirty times its height downwind, but really useful shelter should not be expected beyond about three heights upwind and twenty heights downwind. This means that a properly designed strip of trees 15 metres high (50 feet) should provide useful shelter to about 300 metres downwind and 45 metres upwind. In considering what is 'useful shelter', however, it may be that even a small reduction of wind velocity may be significant in bringing it below some threshold level that is critical for soil erosion or damage to plants. The figures quoted apply where the wind direction is perpendicular to the belt; where the wind strikes the belt obliquely the protected zone is correspondingly reduced.

The shape of the sheltered zone in the lee of a strip of trees is bluntly triangular, since the wind sweeps round the ends of the strip as well as over the top. Strips with a length less than twelve times the height of the trees generally fail to develop the full zone of shelter to leeward, and this presupposes that the wind blows always at right-angles to the length of the belt; allowing for variations in wind direction, it is reasonable to design a belt for crop shelter on the basis of its minimum length being twenty-five times its expected height to allow a fair return on the investment. This would mean a belt 375 metres long if it is expected to be 15 metres high. This relationship however would not apply to shelter blocks for stock (discussed later) nor to situations where the belt is part of a complex or a grid system of shelter strips (Plate 5.1).

Although the extent of shelter is primarily dependent on the tree height, other features of the design of the belt and its structure exert considerable influence, especially its permeability to the wind. A solid or dense barrier is much less efficient for farm shelter than a more open structure which is partly permeable to the wind. Dense shelterbelts provide an intense reduction of the windspeed immediately in their lee but the sheltered zone is terminated quite abruptly by strong down-draughts and eddies which quickly result in the re-establishment of the original windspeed (Figure 5.2). Behind a shelterbelt that is moderately permeable to the wind the greatest shelter is to be found between two and five tree heights downwind from the belt and there is a very gradual restoration of the original free wind velocity (Figure 5.1). A more open-structured belt produces its best shelter further to leeward but with less reduction of the wind speed.

Plate 5.1   A grid system of shelter strips, central Scotland.

The intense reduction of windspeed close to a dense shelterbelt and the narrow zone of effective shelter is generally undesirable for the protection of field crops and of soil against wind erosion. It is also unsuitable for the amelioration of the climate near the ground over a whole district, which the accumulated effect of a landscape of shelterbelts has been shown to produce. This type of shelter, however, may be very suitable for the protection of livestock in severe weather.

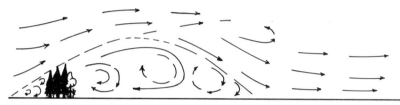

Figure 5.2   Pattern of wind flow over an impermeable shelterbelt: large standing eddies and a very short zone of shelter.

Shelterbelt design and location

Permeability is of outstanding importance in effective shelterbelt design and the optimum degree of permeability or porosity for farm shelterbelts is approximately 40 per cent. In practical terms this means being able to see movement of animals on the other side of a belt but not clearly enough to recognise their identity. The aim should be to achieve this by providing a good distribution of small openings in the belt structure rather than few large ones. Especially undesirable are shelterbelts which are 'porous' simply because the bottom (the bole space) has become open and draughty, since the wind accelerates through these channels and creates harmful conditions for crops, people and stock. The acceleration of the wind through the belt of trees is undesirable not only for its effect on leeward shelter, but also because of the difficulty it imposes on the silvicultural management of the belt itself. When a shelterbelt has become 'leggy' and draughty, it is extremely difficult to grow any young trees or bushes to restore the structure since the high windspeed damages the plants. The maintenance of shrubs as a windward margin or as an understorey within a shelterbelt is especially important in exposed areas.

For a given permeability, the width of a shelterbelt has no appreciable effect on the abatement of the wind flow. A wide impenetrable belt does not produce more shelter than a narrow impenetrable belt; indeed studies have shown that to some extent a wide shelterbelt may 'consume' some of its own shelter and is less efficient than a narrower one. With increasing width it becomes progressively more difficult to achieve 40 per cent penetration by the wind without creating structural weakness which threatens the stability of the whole wood. Much depends on the tree species, but designs of narrow belts, say three, five or seven rows wide, are now seen to be much more efficient for crop shelter than broader belts. Narrow shelterbelts carry the penalty that it is virtually impossible to restore and regenerate them except by complete removal of the trees and replanting, and have higher fencing costs, but this seems preferable to the creation of tree strips that are neither useful for shelter nor effective for timber growing. Narrow belts also have the merit of using less valuable cropping land for tree growth.

Shelterbelts should be designed so that the overhanging of agricultural land is avoided. Direct shading and the dripping of rain water from the tree branches are harmful to the farm crops and reduce crop yields severely: east-west belts especially throw shadow across the fields. The maintenance of a hedge or fringe of shrubs is generally helpful in avoiding the draughty and 'leggy' condition in older belts, and this is made particularly difficult if the main trees are allowed to produce heavy overhanging crowns. For narrow woodland strips (say 20 m wide) where shelter is not the over-riding objective, an A-shaped cross-section with large trees in the central third and smaller broadleaved trees or shrubs in the outer two thirds will overcome many of these problems. (For greatest efficiency the windward edge of a shelterbelt should not be tapered in this way.) If an additional edge strip is left unplanted this will enhance the wildlife value of the strip and permit easier access; the two outer sections can be coppiced alternately to maintain low shelter and provide habitat diversity and firewood.

The longevity of a shelterbelt is of considerable importance. Its main service is the provision of shelter from the wind and it is desirable that it should give that service for a long period without reinvestment, at a slow depreciation rate. The speedy provision of shelter or amenity often results in the planting of a belt which deteriorates rapidly and has soon to be renewed. Good design may allow the use of a very fast-growing species (willow, poplar, Sitka spruce, according to soil and climate) as a temporary screen while slower-growing, longer-lived trees are establishing themselves—an approach similar to using nurse trees as described in Chapter 4 (see page 55).

On the majority of farms where shelterbelts can be useful, the most suitable trees are likely to be, in an ecological sense, pioneer species. Particularly useful are sycamore, sessile oak, lime, Scots pine and Corsican pine, with whitebeam, cherry and rowan as shorter-stature trees, and holly, hazel and hawthorn as shrubs. Where the climate is harsh and at high elevations the useful species include birch, alder, willow and hybrid larch on the more fertile soils and Scots pine, shore pine (*Pinus contorta*) and noble fir (*Abies procera*) on the infertile ones. Sitka spruce is very resistant to wind blast, especially when it is young, and it can provide quick shelter, but it is difficult to maintain it in a narrow strip and to thin it in a wider one to achieve the desired degree of permeability. Some tree species have characteristics making them unsuitable for shelter planting: beech tends to produce heavily branched crowns to leeward, with consequent damage to shrubs and field crops; the long-spreading feeding roots of ash are considered harmful by many farmers; Douglas fir tends to lose its crown in exposed conditions and to become deformed.

The location of shelterbelts is described at the start of Chapter 4 (see page 49).

Shelter on different farm types
In the hills and uplands the most useful shelter may be given by blocks of trees to which livestock can move in severe weather, making no attempt to shelter the grazing (Plate 5.2). The shape of such blocks is generally a simple rectangle although some farmers favour an L-shape, cross or 'Manx leg' design: all these provide some good shelter irrespective of the

Plate 5.2 Location of tree shelter in the uplands: the detached block (upper left) allows stock to find shelter from any wind direction, while gully planting (middle right) reduces the risk of sheep being trapped in snow drifts.

storm direction. The more complicated the shape, the greater the fencing cost, but this may be partly offset by planting tree blocks to divide the hill pasture into paddocks in order to exercise better control of the grazing.

Usually no attempt is made to achieve wind penetrability in storm shelter blocks. It is a positive advantage if the animals are encouraged to congregate in the deep shelter that a dense block provides since they are easier to find and to feed. However, concentration of animals can lead to poaching of the land: this can occur in the lee of any dense blocks or belts where, in addition to heavy trampling, the ground is often partly shaded from the sun and exposed to less wind to dry the soil. The poaching effect is less behind well-designed penetrable shelterbelts, where animals have less reason to congregate in the immediate vicinity of the trees. The same tendencies are evident with regard to flies: numbers are greatest in the calm zone immediately in the lee of dense shelter and animals are less troubled in the moderately breezy conditions behind penetrable shelterbelts.

Sometimes the storm blocks may be usefully located with a view to special hazards for stock on the hill. Outwintered sheep may naturally seek shelter in deep stream gullies which can become dangerous traps because of snow drifting into them (Plate 5.2). Shepherds may be well pleased to see these fenced and planted so that sheep get benefit behind the trees and are kept out of the greater risk.

On some stock farms, especially in the uplands, there is advantage in allowing stock access to woodland for winter shelter. The animals enjoy some of the benefits of being wintered indoors—less loss of body heat than on the open hill and therefore less need for food intake—at a lower cost than building sheds. There may also be the management advantage that the stockman knows where to find the animals and where to take food if there is a severe storm. In the shady conditions of a normal woodland the grass or other ground vegetation seldom has sufficient feeding value to make an appreciable difference to food requirements and the value is principally the reduction in the animals' metabolic stress.

Allowing stock access to woodland also involves costs. If the area is small, as it is likely to be, there is a severe pressure on the soil with continuous trampling which badly affects most trees because their feeding roots are almost at the soil surface. Poor drainage will exacerbate the problem of poaching. Some trees have thin bark which animals enjoy gnawing and which is attractive nutritionally as roughage or moisture when they are being fed on dry concentrate food. Consequently the stock husbandry benefits may be gained at high cost to the woodland. Where a farmer decides to winter stock among the trees he should try to plan for rotational working so that each area is rested and given time to recover, perhaps for two years out of three. During good spells of weather it may be possible to take the stock out of the woodland for a period.

In Chapter 9 reference will be made to agroforestry systems in which farm cropping or grazing is combined with tree growing on the same land. The advantages sought are those of shelter for the animals and reduced climatic stress for them and the plants they eat. The challenge is to discover if a worthwhile crop of trees can be grown while at the same time letting through sufficient light to maintain a productive sward of grass. The dangers of bark gnawing, browsing and soil compaction will all be present, just as in the overwintering situation described above. Success is not a racing certainty, but few things in farming and forestry are.

In the lowlands the objective is likely to be the provision of shelter for whole fields and the constraint on land area used for planting will be greater than in the poorer hills and uplands. Where the crop is predominantly cereals, moderate exposure to wind may be an advantage for drying the grain and, in British conditions where the spreading of winter snow on the land is not crucial, there may be no real advantage in planting shelterbelts. If a farmer wants shelter and timber it is probably best for him to keep these on separate plots of land: plant well-designed belts specifically for shelter (narrow and penetrable, etc.) and grow timber trees in a separate block of woodland.

An important application for the narrowest belts is in orchard management. The objective is to protect the whole fruit crop from gales, especially at blossom time and when the fruit is newly set. A suitable design is virtually a very tall hedge, narrow, so that it uses as little of the valuable land as possible, and penetrable by the wind. Penetrability is highly important because the need is for a general slowing of the windspeed across the whole orchard and, above all, for the eddies and downdraughts of sudden gusts to be avoided. A suitable design which attempts to lift the whole airstream above fruit tree height is to have a series of parallel belts at a spacing of about 25 tree heights, at right angles to the most damaging wind.

In orchards especially, but in virtually all shelterbelt planning, the planter should avoid blocking the natural drainage of cold air on calm nights, as this may create frost pockets and result in more damage than improvement.

Summary guidelines
The following outline summarises the main points to consider when planning and managing shelterbelts.

- **purpose and hence type of shelter that is needed:**
  e.g. narrow zone of maximum shelter for livestock.
  large area of reduced windspeed to reduce soil erosion.

- **design of shelterbelt:**
  'tall hedges' for orchards.
  3–7 row belts for crop shelter (7–15 m wide).
  blocks for storm shelter of livestock (1–10 ha, various shapes).

- **location of shelterbelt:**
  site at regular intervals on flat land; distance = 20 H, where H is the height of mature trees.
  take account of topography in hilly land.
  avoid poorly drained sites for stability.
  beware of shading crops and buildings.

- **establishment and maintenance of trees:**
  species—consider the preceding points, along with general and local site conditions.
  use closer spacing in uplands (1.6–1.8 m).
  take extra care in ground preparation, protection and weeding to ensure good establishment.
  trim hedges (if present) to retain low shelter.
  no brashing!
  thin cautiously to retain permeability (not applicable to shelter blocks).

- **replacement of shelterbelt:**
  clearfell and replant narrow belts—ideally, establish new belts at half rotation age.
  fell and restock (or coppice) alternate halves of wider (20–30 m) strips.

Snow Drifting

On the wheatlands of the Great Plains of the USA and on the steppes of the Soviet Union, shelterbelts may improve crop yields significantly. There cereal yields are critically affected in the early summer by soil moisture which, in turn, depends on the distribution of winter snow. In effect, the benefit of the penetrable shelterbelts is to ensure that snow lies evenly over the partly sheltered field and that it remains there until the spring melt.

The same principles govern the design of snow-fences to protect lines of communication and the layout of shelterbelts for crops and stock. The semi-permeable screen promotes the even spread of snow in the leeward field. In contrast, a dense barrier will cause the snow to be deposited and to accumulate in the narrow zone of intense shelter in, or close to, the barrier itself. Consequently, it is especially undesirable, in a locality where heavy drifting of snow is a recurring problem, to site a shelterbelt close alongside a road. It is fairly common for roads which are flanked by large hedges to become blocked with drifted snow, while the neighbouring fields have been blown completely clear. The solution, adopted by some local authorities, may be to plant a shelter strip 30 to 50 metres back from the road, so that the trees form a still-air zone there in which snow lodges, with the road itself in a wind-eddy acceleration zone which is continually swept clear.

The design of strips to act as snow traps is complicated by the nature of the vegetation on the open ground nearby. Short-cropped grass, fallow and autumn-sown cereals do not readily hold snow, and they tend to be easily blown clear, thus providing more snow for drifting. In contrast, old deep heather and winter vegetable crops hold large amounts of snow and tend to reduce the local drifting problem. In consequence, it is difficult to provide simple, widely applicable designs; the local conditions, both topographical and vegetational, exert powerful influences.

A tree strip which has been successful in acting as a snow trap may suffer from bark damage by sheep or deer enabled to gain access over the fence (Plate 5.3).

OTHER PRODUCTS AND EFFECTS OF WOODLAND

The physical effects of trees on the farm climate are often uppermost in the minds of farmers who are thinking about planting trees for the first time. However, other aspects, including woodland products, are also important; the rest of this chapter mentions these briefly and concludes with the results of a recent survey that examined the differences in attitude to farm woodlands among farmers who do and do not have trees on their farm.

Firewood

A significant benefit of existing woods and those planted for non-timber objectives comes from the timber produced. Despite rural electrification and the national grid, many farmhouses still have open fires and many farms have installed bale burners or woodburning stoves for central- or water-heating purposes. A few afternoons' work in winter may contribute considerably to reduced electricity bills. Existing areas of

Plate 5.3   Sheep damage at 1–2 metres above ground level due to snow drifts in the lee of a shelterbelt.

neglected coppice (Plate 5.4) will yield adequate wood for this purpose provided their future is planned for sustained production: this could mean the resumption of coppicing, or restocking by planting or natural regeneration. Heating for a typical house requires 4–5 hectares of coppice to provide fuelwood in perpetuity (see page 32). In the enthusiasm of reducing electricity bills it is important that the farm is not stripped of trees and future wood production sacrificed as firewood.

Other Wood Products

Other uses for farm timber include strainers and fence posts, although the cost of the various fencing options needs to be considered carefully. If labour availability for fencing is scarce, untreated posts needing frequent renewal may not turn out to be such a good idea as they seemed at first. However, in West Germany and other parts of Europe it is quite common to see gates, fences and indeed the framework of farm buildings made out of timber produced on the farm (Plate 5.5). This is undoubtedly a subject worth exploring further in Britain.

Plate 5.4 Birch coppice suitable for firewood if cut on a thirty-year rotation.

Plate 5.5 Roof timbers cut from trees grown on the farm (West Germany).

Shooting

Another popular byproduct of woodland on the farm is the cover provided for game birds. If shooting is a priority and is to be one of the main pleasures obtained from the trees then the Game Conservancy or the British Association for Shooting and Conservation should be consulted (addresses in Appendix 3). If your aim is to gain a bit of rough shooting, then, provided some undergrowth is maintained once the trees have become established, the trees themselves will provide this.

Landscape and Amenity

Attitudes to trees vary as widely among farmers as among any other group within the community. The impact of trees, though impossible to measure, must be a major factor in the daily lives of farmers and farmworkers. What would the place be like if all the trees were felled tomorrow? This thought itself may be sufficient to ensure that steps are taken which guarantee that future generations also enjoy the presence of trees on the land, although amenity benefits, *per se*, are rarely enough to result in planting, except perhaps about the house and steading. It is important that the design of the woodland and its context on the farm should be considered as a whole in order to avoid, as far as can be, the disappointment and problems of conflicting objectives. Even a beautiful wood may bring problems if the general public who walk in it leave rubbish and open gates in their wake. It is also important to remember that farm woods and trees should look 'right' as part of the overall landscape (see page 5).

Problems Associated with Trees

In some farmers' minds trees and woods are associated with farm pests: foxes, rabbits, pigeons, rooks and crows, flies and deer. Trees provide cover and can provide new breeding areas so that in time control may become necessary; this appears to be particularly true on farms where large areas of conifers have been planted.

It is in the farmer's own interest, and neighbourly, that these potential troublemakers be kept in check. This control is made easier in managed woodland since management provides necessary access and familiarity with the woods and the creatures in them. Collaboration among groups of landowners is important: all should be aware of the needs of sheep-farming neighbours in respect of fox control, and joint action should be taken against rabbits and other pests. It would certainly be an error to invest heavily in planting woodland and then merely hope that damaging animals will keep away. The fact that pigeons find sowings of winter barley and woodland roosting sites close together will virtually ensure their presence. Generally a natural balance between these populations will be arrived at, with foxes and crows controlling rabbits and other small mammals; the attempted obliteration of rabbits may result in hungry predators which might not be the desired result at all!

Trees can present other difficulties in association with crop husbandry. Shallow-rooting species, such as ash, in hedgerows can cause problems for ploughing (the roots may also be severed which damages the tree) and the 'debris' dropped during storms can cause damage to machinery. Crops growing under overhanging trees may develop a water-deficit, shading may delay drying and the lodging caused by eddies of air in fields of ripening grain is well known. This underlines the need for intelligent planning. The right species must be planted and managed in the correct way so that the farm as a whole benefits from the woodland enterprise. This is borne out by the results of the survey reported in the next section.

RESULTS OF A SURVEY OF FARMERS

The decisions taken by farmers in planting and managing woodland are greatly influenced by what they hope and expect trees may provide. In 1984 and 1985 more than two thousand farmers in northern England and Scotland were approached to discover their attitudes to woodlands on the farm. The survey aimed to examine the issues most commonly believed to concern farmers and this was followed up by extended interviews with a sample of farmers who had direct experience of farm trees and woods.

It seemed likely that farmers with trees on their land would be aware of different things from those with no trees. The mail survey first established whether or not the farms had any trees on them and, if so, whether these were few and scattered, such as parkland or hedgerow trees, or were areas of woodland. The woodlands ranged from 'pocket handkerchiefs' in field corners to a small number of substantial commercial enterprises.

For all the factors surveyed, farmers with trees and woods were, as expected, more aware of both their advantages and disadvantages. For instance, 38 per cent of all farmers who answered the question said that private shooting was a relevant factor in deciding to maintain or create farm woodlands; among farmers with no trees at all that percentage was only 20, whereas among those with woodlands (however large or small) it was 55 (see Table 5.1.)

Table 5.1. Response to questionnaire on benefits and disadvantages of farm woodlands: percentage of farmers replying that particular factors were relevant

Factor	All farms	No trees	Farms with woods
Benefits			
Private shooting	38	20	55
Firewood production	65	60	76
Control of snow drift	48	34	53
Crop shelter	47	33	52
Steading shelter	64	44	70
Stock shelter	73	32	79
Pleasure for farmer	68	45	75
Landscape value	77	50	85
Wildlife habitats	77	56	86
Disadvantages			
Worse snow drifting	32	25	36
Financial costs	36	20	42
Crop lodging	41	29	45
Crop shading	54	35	59
Leaves, debris, etc.	54	36	58
Foxes, rabbits, etc.	65	45	72
Flies	69	51	75

From M.Phil. thesis by C. Sidwell.

When the figures for disadvantages are examined in the table, it seems that the difference between the opinions of farmers with and without trees is rather small, except in regard to pests such as foxes, rabbits and pigeons, which are clearly associated with trees. In some instances, however, there had been a problem with rabbits or foxes before the trees were planted, and the woods were created on particular sites in an effort to minimise agricultural losses.

Flies represented the largest problem associated with woodlands, although the stock farmers indicated that the provision of shelter placed the balance of advantage in favour of having trees. The worst problems with head flies were avoided by keeping stock on the more exposed pastures in summer and allowing them access to the strip beside shelter only in severe weather. Even on dairy farms, where the problems of summer mastitis are often believed to be a major deterrent to tree planting, the number of farmers who benefited from shelter exceeded the number suffering from fly problems.

For each farm type the number of farmers who said that they benefited overall from the trees on the farm exceeded the number who said that they did not. On the other hand, the number of farmers who felt that they suffered from neighbours' woodlands adjoining their land exceeded the number who said they had benefited from them. The need for good management and neighbourliness is emphasised in this result.

A notable and unexpected feature of the survey results was the balance of interest among farmers between production benefits and non-market benefits. As mentioned previously, the interest in private shooting was relatively low—38 per cent overall and only a little over half on farms with woodlands. Firewood production (65 per cent), crop shelter (47 per cent) and stock shelter (73 per cent) were all markedly higher. The factors attracting the highest interest and those considered most relevant in deciding on the creation or maintenance of woodland were landscape value (77 per cent) and provision of wildlife habitats (77 per cent), with the farmer's own interest and pleasure (68 per cent) only slightly behind.

Chapter 6

THE INSTITUTIONAL ENVIRONMENT

It has already been stressed that in planning to manage existing woodlands or to create new ones it is necessary to decide on the objectives and priorities for each wood and to consider both local site conditions and broader environmental issues. This, however is only part of the picture. A third element, which has been touched on briefly in Chapter 4, relates to the land use environment in which the farm is found. If the farm is in a National Park, for instance, there may be certain things the farmer is prohibited from doing; there will also be some things which are encouraged and others which are not. This chapter aims to give a brief history of those Government agencies involved in land designation for various purposes, and to describe both the areas affected and the restrictions on land use activities found in them. The addresses of the agencies can be found in Appendix 3.

AGENCIES INVOLVED IN LAND USE

The Countryside Commission (CC)

The Countryside Commission was created in 1968 to replace the National Parks Commission. The latter had been created under the 1949 National Parks and Access to the Countryside Act (the 1949 Act) which charged it with the following objectives:

- preserving and enhancing the natural beauty of England and Wales, particularly in the areas designated as National Parks or Areas of Outstanding Natural Beauty (AONB).

- encouraging the provision or improvement of facilities for people using the National Parks for open-air recreation and the study of nature.

The National Parks Commission was also expected to keep both recreation within the Parks and conservation of natural beauty under review; to communicate with and guide the planning authorities in order to achieve any necessary changes; and to facilitate administration. Where more than one planning authority was involved, a joint planning board was established. Where only a single authority was concerned a separate sub-committee of the planning board was convened to consider planning decisions within the Park area.

The Countryside Commission, like the earlier Commission, has responsibility for providing recreation facilities in the National Parks and for preserving and enhancing the natural beauty of the countryside in England. Prior to April 1991 the Commission's responsibility extended to Wales but from that date, in accordance with the Environmental Protection Act 1990, the Welsh division of the CC was hived off and merged with the Welsh element of the Nature Conservancy Council to form a new agency, the Countryside Council for Wales. Since April 1991, the Countryside Commission's remit has been for England only.

The CC is charged with:

- providing and improving facilities for the enjoyment of the countryside;

- conserving and enhancing the natural beauty and amenity of the countryside;

- reviewing the need to secure public access to the countryside for the purpose of open-air recreation;

- making recommendations concerning by-laws;

- creating experimental projects and schemes to illustrate the appropriateness of new techniques and concepts;

- giving advice and making recommendations to the Minister, particularly relating to the decisions concerning the development of land within the National Parks.

The CC gives some grants for amenity tree planting (see Chapter 7) and is responsible for assessment of land for certain tax reliefs (in return for management agreements) where they agree that the land is of particular scenic value. The Commission's central office is at Cheltenham (see Appendix 3 for address).

The Countryside Commission for Scotland (CCS)

The Countryside Commission for Scotland was established in 1967 by the Countryside (Scotland) Act. It had not been considered appropriate to include Scotland under the provisions of the 1949 Act, since the size and mobility of the population appeared less threatening to Scotland's countryside at that time than in England and Wales. As a result, the National Parks Commission never had any jurisdiction within Scotland.

By 1967 it had become clear that it would be necessary to protect Scotland's countryside and to provide access to it for the urban-based population. The Commission's office is at Battleby, near Perth (see Appendix 3). The 1967 Act envisaged that the Countryside Commission for Scotland would enable the

- provision, development and improvement of facilities for the enjoyment of the Scottish countryside and for the conservation of the natural beauty and amenity thereof,

whilst giving

- due regard to the need for the development of recreational and tourist facilities and for the balanced economic and social development of the countryside.

The CCS has the power to give a variety of grants to organisations and individuals, as well as to designate various types of park (Regional, Country), and it has the following statutory obligations:

- to review the matters outlined above;
- to encourage and assist in the implementation of proposals to achieve them;
- to exercise functions relating to the development of special projects and schemes;
- to consult local planning authorities about their responsibilities with regard to the countryside;
- to advise the Secretary of State on matters relating to the countryside.

The Countryside Commission for Scotland promotes and assists in the provision of recreation facilities and the conservation of natural beauty and amenity, by means of grants, research, education and publicity. It offers grants for amenity planting of trees and for establishing improved access (stiles, footpaths and footbridges) and is involved in farm open days for the public, offering advice, help and training for those wishing to provide facilities for visitors to the countryside. It is also involved in assessment of Inheritance Tax Relief for areas of scenic importance.

With new legislation before Parliament in 1991, the Government plans to merge the CCS with the Nature Conservancy Council for Scotland (NCCS) to form a new agency, Scottish Natural Heritage (SNH), with effect from April 1992. (See Nature Conservancy below).

Nature Conservancy and its Successor Agencies

The Nature Conservancy was originally established in 1948 and given enhanced powers under the 1949 Act. Its structure and responsibilities were changed in 1973 and from that date to 1991 it operated as the Nature Conservancy Council throughout Great Britain. Its role and powers were much extended by the Wildlife and Countryside Act 1981.

By various Acts, the NCC was empowered to establish and manage nature reserves, to designate Sites of Special Scientific Interest and to enter into management agreements with the owners of the land on which these reserves and sites lie. It was obliged to notify the appropriate local authority of the existence of the nature reserves and safeguarded sites in order that they might incorporate the information into their planning framework, and also to notify the landowners and occupiers.

The NCC was responsible for provision of advice to Government Ministers about the development and implementation of policies relating to nature conservation in Great Britain and also for the initiation of relevant research and the dissemination of information and advice to the general public. The Council was also responsible for the designation of Sites of Special Scientific Interest (SSSIs) and for notifying the owners and occupiers of such land that it had been classified in that way. (Further details are given on p. 94–95, 111.)

The passing of the Environmental Protection Act 1990 resulted in the division of the Nature Conservancy Council into three country agencies as from April 1991: the Nature Conservancy Council for England, the Nature Conservancy Council for Scotland and the Countryside Council for Wales. The Countryside Council for Wales was formed by the amalgamation of the NCC in Wales with the Countryside Commission's Welsh division.

The successor agencies in each country, and their equivalent newly

formed in Northern Ireland, are responsible to their respective Sec-
retaries of State (i.e. of the Environment of Scotland, of Wales and
of Northern Ireland). In all cases the successor agency inherits all
the powers and responsibilities of the former NCC, with enhanced
funding.

It is expected that the NCC for Scotland will have a short life
as a separate agency. The Natural Heritage (Scotland) Bill would,
on enactment, merge the NCC for Scotland with the Countryside
Commission for Scotland in April 1992, to create the new agency,
Scottish Natural Heritage (SNH) which would inherit all the former
NCC's duties and all CCS's; in addition, SNH would have the power
to designate heritage areas, similar to the Countryside Commission's
powers to create National Parks and Areas of Outstanding Natural
Beauty in England.

The NCC's successor agencies jointly fund and service the Joint
Nature Conservation Committee (JNCC) to coordinate their practices
and to discharge their international conservation responsibilities on
behalf of the UK.

Successor agencies offer grants for tree planting for conservation
purposes (see Chapter 7) and have local field officers who are able to
help with advice for both tree planting and other amenity or ecological
innovations such as creating ponds and establishing appropriate cover
around them. If you have woods on the farm that are known to have
existed for generations and you wish to maintain their character, or if
you want to encourage wildlife in the woods, these officers are likely
to be the most appropriate source of management advice.

Forestry Commission (FC)

The Forestry Commission is the principal support agency concerning
trees and woodlands. It was established in 1919, in the aftermath of
the First World War, when it had become apparent that the lack
of home-grown timber might put Britain at risk in the event of
another war, particularly because of the commitment of shipping
capacity that timber imports would need. The FC has a twofold
function:

- as 'Forestry Enterprise', the FC is responsible for developing and
  managing its forest resource, including the acquisition and planting
  of land for the production of timber.

- as 'Forestry Authority' the FC is responsible for the administration
  of government grants to both private individuals and companies

who undertake tree planting. It is also responsible for the granting of felling licences and carries out much of the forestry research in Great Britain. It is the national authority for the co-ordination of all forestry affairs, statistics and the representation of forestry at Ministerial level.

The FC grant schemes are described, with others, in Chapter 7. It should be pointed out that, as well as administering grants, the FC has Private Woodlands Officers in each Conservancy (addresses in Appendix 3) who give free advice on all aspects of woodland work. The rules concerning felling licences granted by the Forestry Commission and the granting of clearance for planting land are referred to in Chapter 7.

Local Authorities

Although Forestry and woodland planting unlike urban building development does not come under planning control, it is worth noting that there are various circumstances when the policy of the Local Authority will determine the outcome of grant applications, amongst other things. In particular the existence, in Scotland, of an Indicative Forest Strategy (see p. 117) will be important as will the location of Regional Parks. In Scotland the Central Scotland Woodland Trust is a special planning area which may prove to be a forerunner of the urban forests currently being mooted by the Countryside Commission in England. Some local authorities may also offer free tree schemes, or woodland management services, often through divisions of their planning departments.

AREAS WHERE LAND USE MAY BE RESTRICTED

The National Parks

The National Parks are perhaps the best known of the areas where restrictions operate. There are seven of them in England (Peak District, Yorkshire Dales, Lake District, Northumberland, North Yorkshire Moors, Exmoor and Dartmoor) and three in Wales (Snowdonia, Pembrokeshire Coast, and Brecon Beacons). The Norfolk Broads Area, although not a National Park, has recently been given special status and now has its own Planning board. There are no National Parks in Scotland where the population density, except in the central belt, is so much less than in the southern part of Britain that it was not felt necessary to nominate specific areas of great scenic beauty for recreation at the time of the Parks' establishment. This is now being reviewed, however, and areas subject to planning restrictions in Scotland are discussed later in this chapter.

The power to create National Parks was established under the 1949 Act. National Parks contain extensive tracts of open country which it was thought would afford opportunity for open-air recreation. They were chosen for their 'natural beauty' and easy access from centres of population, and now cover 9.5 per cent of the area of England and Wales (13,600 km²).

Farmers within a National Park can be asked to enter into access agreements where the land is open, or be served with access orders obliging them to maintain the land in a condition that allows access where this is not the case. No work is allowed that will substantially reduce access except for short periods when advance notice must be given. The 1976 restatement of objectives by the Countryside Commission emphasises that conservation of beauty and ecological considerations should take priority in all matters, including roads, traffic and the provision of tourist facilities. It also recognises the importance of agriculture and woodlands within the Parks and the need both to protect farmers and other land-owners from the pressures created by visitors and to help them cope with such pressures, although this point has never been reinforced by legislation.

There is a presumption against any development considered to be out of accord with the purposes of a National Park, which may in some cases amount to a virtual prohibition on building development. The restrictions that exist vary from one park to another according to the decisions made by the joint planning boards, which are representative of the different local authorities who have planning control in the area. In general, building is more tightly controlled than in other parts of the country and tree planting (particularly afforestation) is also more tightly controlled by a voluntary agreement to refer grant applications to the planning authority concerned. The intention of this is to maintain the character of the area which could easily be damaged by poor design or inappropriate planting. The corollary to restrictions that may exist to prevent indiscriminate tree planting is that there are often incentives, in the form of grants, to encourage land owners to plant 'permitted' trees. It may be possible to achieve shelter planting in exposed sites through the traditional method of planting a mixture of species and taking out the conifers as thinnings in the early years. However this depends on the locality and on the particular planning authority concerned.

Areas of Outstanding Natural Beauty (AONBs)

The concept of Areas of Outstanding Natural Beauty was defined in the 1949 Act and relates largely to landscape and amenity, although the fauna and flora of an area are included in addition to geological and physiographic features. The Countryside Commission designates an area which must then be approved for AONB status by the Secretary of State for the Environment. The AONBs are mainly areas of outstanding local value, but which are not suitable for National Park designation due to the lack of open country and scope for large-scale recreation. Although access is not an objective of AONB status the Countryside Commission will encourage attempts to provide access within these areas. There have been no National Parks or AONBs in Scotland prior to 1991, although the Natural Heritage (Scotland) Bill may well provide powers for the SNH to designate these or areas with a very similar purpose.

There are currently thirty-eight AONBs in England and Wales, covering 11.3 per cent of the land area (17,084 km^2) with nine in Northern Ireland and another six proposed. It is important to know if the farm is within an AONB as this has the following implications:

- it is unlikely that any government or other public agency will propose new reservoirs, power stations or major roads in an AONB;

- AONB designation strengthens the hand of local planning authorities in rejecting new urban development proposals;

- AONB status encourages the appointment of ranger services;

- AONB status makes funds for conservation more likely to be available from both the local authority, local naturalists' trusts and the CC;

- AONB status increases the likelihood that Inheritance Tax (previously Capital Transfer Tax) relief will be available.

For farmers interested in tree planting the consequence is likely to be that consultation procedures involved in Forestry Commission grant applications may result in refusal of permission for large areas of coniferous planting. However broadleaved woodlands applications to both the FC and CC are likely to be approved for grant. The existence of CC rangers may also result in an additional source of advice for the farmer, although their primary objective is to assist with the provision of access. Grants for footpaths and stiles are likely to be readily available in these areas, either from the local authority or the Countryside

Commission. From April 1991 these arrangements are operated by the CC for Wales.

Scottish Designations including National Scenic Areas (NSAs)

National Scenic Areas have replaced the five National Park Direction Areas that had existed since 1948. There are 40 NSAs covering a total of 13 per cent of the Scottish Land area and they are described as being areas of locally outstanding scenic value which are of national importance. Planning restrictions will operate in these areas and all applications for development must be submitted to the Secretary of State.

The Countryside (Scotland) Act 1967 allowed the creation of Country Parks, which are intended to afford the public opportunities for the enjoyment of the countryside and open-air recreation. Although there is some farming activity within these areas they are, in the main, fairly small areas owned by the local authority which may lease fields to local farmers. Recreation is the main priority and therefore farming operations will be restricted if necessary.

In 1981 an addition to the 1967 Act allowed the designation, by Regional Councils, of Regional Parks. Like the National Parks in England and Wales, these are administered for planning purposes as one unit and are extensive areas of land. Part of each Park is devoted to the recreational needs of the public. The same Act allowed the introduction of management agreements in areas of local importance, which help to reduce conflict and minimise the pressure on farmers and landowners. In the Pentland Hills in Lothian Region, an area of special planning control was drawn up where the CCS had to be consulted over some categories of development proposals. Since the autumn of 1986 this area has been a Regional Park.

A further development in Scotland has been the formulation by a number of Local Authorities of what have become known as 'Indicative Forest Strategies'. These determine areas where forestry may be considered an appropriate form of development and those where it may be discouraged within the Region. They are dealt with more fully on p. 117.

'Areas of Great Landscape Value' may be designated by local planning authorities in their Development Plans. Although these may allow some control over development they are not standard across Scotland.

Scottish Natural Heritage will inherit all the powers of CCS, plus some others, and these arrangements should not be expected to weaken.

Countryside designations in Scotland are currently under review, particularly with regard to popular mountain areas which are now under increasingly heavy pressure. Many landowners agree that some form of protection is necessary, but do not wish to see any statutory designation of their area (be it called a National Park or some other name) which might, by concentrating visitor pressure, create 'honey-pot' problems that Scotland has largely managed to avoid so far.

Nature Reserves

The NCC's successor agencies have a statutory obligation to establish, maintain and manage nature reserves. The purpose of the reserves is to protect the most important features of the different habitats (including flora, fauna and geological or physiographic features) found within the area and to maintain the diversity currently found in Great Britain, whilst realising their potential for research and education.

There are 121 National Nature Reserves (NNR) in England, 45 in Wales and 68 in Scotland covering total areas of approximately 41,000, 12,000 and 112,000 ha respectively. Only 13 per cent of the land in NNR is owned by the conservation agencies and they have long-term leases on a further 27 per cent. The remaining 60 per cent is owned by other interests so that the Councils must work with private landowners and occupiers, through management agreements, to ensure that it is managed in the 'national interest'. These agreements are designed to allow agricultural operations within the constraints necessary for the proper protection of the nature reserve. They may contain restrictions on the work carried out on the land but there may be compensation for the cost of such restrictions. If the conservation agency is not convinced that the management agreement will be adhered to, or if it has previously been ignored, they may compulsorily purchase the land. The conservation agency may make by-laws to protect the reserve which they have created. Local authorities also have the power to create nature reserves within their own area of jurisdiction. Details of relevant legislation (in the Wildlife and Countryside Act) are covered in Chapter 7.

Some UK reserves are internationally significant. These include RAMSAR sites (30 wetland sites in the UK designated in accordance with the RAMSAR convention) and Biosphere sites (13 areas notified to the UK by UNESCO).

The European Community has designated Special Protection Areas, which are established by member states to conserve endangered species of birds, those with restricted local populations, or requiring special habitat protection. Twenty two such areas have been notified to the European Commission by the UK Government.

It is worth pointing out that nature conservation and commercial woodland are not necessarily mutually exclusive. For example, over half of the British butterfly species—including some rarities—can be found in a Forestry Commission plantation near Oxford, where special rideside management has been agreed.

Sites of Special Scientific Interest (SSSI)

Sites of Special Scientific Interest are designated by the NCC and its successor agencies. They contain features of local or national rarity and are therefore of special scientific interest. They are protected because intensive agricultural, mining or forestry activity might destroy the features of interest and both the origin and the future of such sites are of importance for scientific research.

A farm SSSI may, for instance, contain meadow or woodland plant species that are rare in the United Kingdom, or unusual in the local area. Not all SSSIs are created for biological reasons; geologically unusual sites (such as features of glaciation) may also be designated and such sites often occur in areas of the farm where agricultural productivity is limited anyway. When the owner is 'notified' of the existence of the site there may be a number of operations which are restricted without prior consultation with the NCC's successor agencies. The owner will be sent a list of 'potentially damaging operations' (PDOs), such as drainage of grassland or overwintering of stock in woodland, which apply in each case. The farmer can then apply for consent to carry out such operations, if any of the PDOs are part of his normal work, so that a suitable management regime can be agreed. Thereafter he must apply for permission each time he intends to carry out any operation not included in the original consent.

Within an SSSI, all grant applications to the Forestry Commission are referred to the NCC's successor body. Often the new planting will not be acceptable but natural regeneration of indigenous species will be eligible and certain operations or changes of land use may be restricted. It should be borne in mind that such restrictions will only apply over that part of the farm which is designated as an SSSI, and the restrictions vary according to the scientific interest that has been notified to the owner and occupier.

Almost all the SSSIs that exist have now been notified to the owner, since the passing of the 1981 Wildlife and Countryside Act. However, if there is some feature of interest within the area in which work is intended, a check should be made with the local office of the

NCC of England, the Countryside Council for Wales, the NCC for Scotland or the SNH to ensure that interesting plants or animals are not overlooked. The local conservation officer will be pleased to help any farmer considering planting trees and may prove to be a useful source of information concerning local people who can give other help or advice.

Environmentally Sensitive Areas (ESAs)

There was considerable publicity over the first designations by Agriculture Departments, in March 1987, of Environmentally Sensitive Areas in England and Wales. The areas now incorporated in England and Wales are:

Breckland	The Broads
The Cambrian Mountains	Lleyn Peninsular
North Peak	The Pennine Dales
Shropshire Borders	Somerset Levels and Moors
The South Downs	Suffolk River Valleys
The Test Valley	West Penwith

Five ESAs have been designated in Scotland to date. These are in the Breadalbane area, Loch Lomond, The Machair lands of the Uists and Benbecula in the Hebrides, Whitlaw-Eildon in the Borders and the Loch Ken and River Dee area in Galloway. The Glens of Antrim, and Mourn and Slievecroob are the two areas designated in Northern Ireland.

The reasons for designation differ in each case and for this reason the preferred management strategy will vary. Within an ESA, farmers are asked to volunteer to enter into management agreements to follow traditional farming practices and to avoid the more intensive agricultural techniques. Those who agree to do so are eligible for special grants and other payments. These agreements will have different management objectives in each of the areas, according to the nature of the site. It may be that tree planting (particularly large scale) is considered likely to upset the balance of the area and to be contrary to the voluntary management agreement, or there may be restrictions on the type of planting that you can carry out. In the Breadalbane area of Scotland, for example, regeneration of birch woodland is a specific objective of the scheme and in many areas management and revitalisation of woodland is encouraged.

If your farm is within an ESA there will probably have been both publicity about the designation in the local press and meetings to give details of how farmers will be affected. The local ADAS office or, in Scotland, College of Agriculture will be able to give you relevant details.

Protection of Archaeological Monuments

The most common form of legal protection given to the field monuments in the UK is 'scheduling', under the terms of the Ancient Monuments and Archaeological Areas Act 1979. In essence, the effect of scheduling is to restrict any works which might take place, requiring the prior consent of the Secretary of State to be obtained. Amongst the most damaging operations are those involving a change of land use, particularly forestry and ploughing up permanent or rough pasture, although other works can be as damaging. Even grazing stock can cause erosion and therefore damage to a site. Drainage and fencing are a problem and all stages of forestry operations, even handplanted trees, cause damage in the long term. Scheduled monument consent can be refused, or granted, subject to conditions. The penalty for damage, for unauthorised works or for breaching the conditions of a consent, is a fine or imprisonment. The responsibility for maintaining a scheduled monument lies with the owner of the land, although he or she is not obliged to maintain it. Management agreements and sometimes grants are available for repairs or the sympathetic management of monuments. Management agreements may also be available for monuments not scheduled.

Grant applications for the Woodland Grant Scheme and for the Farm Woodland Scheme require the identification of any ancient monument or archaeological site, (whether or not scheduled) and their exclusion from areas to be planted. All applications for grant are notified to the County Archaeologist or Regional Archaeologist in Scotland (where one is in post) or Historic Buildings and Monuments, Scotland, to identify areas of archaeological interest (whether or not they are scheduled) which should be left unplanted.

The protection of monuments or areas of archaeological interest may also be a factor in exemption from Capital Transfer Tax.

References for further reading
See Appendix 2.

Chapter 7

FINANCE, TAXATION AND LAW

After the neglect of forestry throughout the nineteenth century, it has been the policy of successive British governments since 1919 to expand tree planting and to improve forest management. The case for increased timber growing is a strong one. Britain now imports about 90 per cent of the wood and wood products we use, at a cost in foreign currency of over £7000 million annually. Over the past sixty years governments have adopted three main ways of promoting this continuing national forest policy:

- the Forestry Commission has bought land to make state forests;
- advice and direct grants have been provided to encourage land-owners, including farmers, to plant their land and to manage plantations effectively, particularly for timber production;
- arrangements have been made through the tax system to make afforestation an especially attractive investment, again with the principal objective of producing timber. The 1988 Budget, however, removed the incentive provided by income tax remission.

The first of those actions has created the large area of forests which are in national ownership. Over the years the second method appealed especially to the traditional estate owners, mainly through the Dedication Scheme which was introduced in 1946. A major national objective at the end of the Second War was to rehabilitate the country's private woodlands which had been heavily felled for timber production in wartime. In the next twenty years more than 500,000 hectares of private forest were planted through the Dedication Scheme; that has now been closed and replaced by the Woodland Grant Scheme and the Farm Woodland Scheme. The third method of encouraging afforestation, mainly through the operation of the income tax regulations, was the foundation of the major forestry investment companies; as will be explained, the incentive offered through income tax remission was removed in the 1988 Finance Act, although neither capital nor income tax effects should be neglected by those already with woodland or considering tree planting.

These ways of promoting forestry have been extremely effective in creating the country's larger production forests, but they have had relatively little effect on farm-forestry. In Britain there is not a strong tradition of forestry amongst farmers, in sharp contrast to the position on the continent of Europe, in Scandinavia and North America, where many farmers expect to engage in their own woodland operations and, in some instances, to draw a significant part of their farm income from wood production.

There are many possible reasons for British farmers not expecting to engage in forestry. The traditional system of tenanted farms on large estates was the normal style of land tenure until a few decades ago (65 per cent of holdings pre-1940, now only 30 per cent). Under this system the tenant farmer crops the fields but the woodlands are usually kept 'in hand' by the estate owner, both for wood production and, more commonly in some parts of the country, for game shooting. This system separated the farmer from interest in the woods and effectively prevented him from gaining experience of forestry operations. Over most of the country, the terms of their tenancies positively dissuaded tenant farmers from farm-forestry, even from the planting of shelterbelts.

It is not difficult to see the reason for a landlord's concern at tenants undertaking tree planting. The capital value of a standing tree crop could build up to £5,000 or £10,000 per hectare, considerably more than the value of the land itself. Because a tenant generally has the right to be compensated through an outgoing valuation for fixed improvements he has made during his tenancy, the landlord might find himself committed to very large capital payments. Many tenant farmers undoubtedly feel that this is a damaging and unnecessary constraint. The fact that, by law, tenants now enjoy much greater security of tenure, even over successive generations, gives weight to the view (which is now evolving) that tree planting should be treated as an exceptional improvement and made the subject of special arrangements between landlord and tenant, so that both may benefit. The possibilities now emerging for lowland farmers to grow broadleaved crops on short rotations give point to these arguments.

Table 7.1 Grants for Farm Woodlands

Funding organisation	Purpose	Title and page reference
Forestry Commission	Timber production, landscape enhancement, wildlife habitats, recreation, restocking existing woods	Woodland Grant Scheme (WGS): capital planting grants in 3 instalments; arable land supplement and Oct. '87 storm damage payment (see page 100).
Forestry Commission jointly with the Agriculture Depts. (MAFF, SOAFD & WOAD)	New woodlands on farms for almost all purposes	Farm Woodland Scheme (FWS): (a) capital planting grants in 3 instalments (b) annual payments (see p. 102).
Forestry Commission jointly with the Agriculture Depts. (MAFF, SOAFD & WOAD)	Withdrawal of land from some arable crops plus new woodland	Set-aside Scheme with Trees *Option 1*: Direct set-aside to Woodland (a) Capital grant as in Woodland Grant Scheme, plus (b) Set-Aside payments for 5 yrs (see page 104). *Option 2*: Set-aside through Farm Woodland Scheme (a) capital grant as in FWS (see page 104). (b) annual grants as in FWS (see page 104)
Agriculture Depts. (MAFF, SOAFD & WOAD)	Hedgerow trees and shelterbelts	Farm & Conservation Grant Scheme; grants for hedges Environmentally Sensitive Area Schemes (ESAs).
Countryside Commission (E & W) and Countryside Commission for Scotland	Amenity, natural beauty and public enjoyment	Amenity Tree Planting Grants (see page 106).
National Park Authorities (E & W only)	Amenity	Financial aid for tree planting and woodland management in National Parks only (see page 107).
Nature Conservancy Council	Wildlife conservation	Grants for planting and management of small woods for wildlife (see page 107).
Woodland Trust	Public access and conservation	Leasing and purchase of semi-natural woodland for conservation.
Tree Council	Amenity and conservation	Grants up to 50% for approved work (see page 107).
Local Authorities	Amenity and access	Grants (varying rates) and other aid.

GRANT SCHEMES

The most important grants available to those who intend to create woodland where timber production is one of the main objectives are those from the Forestry Commission, and indeed they are likely to be financially the most attractive in most circumstances even when the principal objective of the tree planting is other than timber. It is quite acceptable that a farmer should apply to the Forestry Commission for a grant when wood production is not his main objective.

The rates of grant are correct at the time of printing but may be revised.

THE WOODLAND GRANT SCHEME (WGS)

As well as timber production, acceptable objectives include landscape enhancement, wildlife habitat improvement, public recreation, game shooting improvement and restocking existing woods. The completed application form, which is available from the local Forestry Commission Conservancy office, must be accompanied by a Plan of Operations covering a five year period, showing what is proposed in creating and managing the woodland. If the proposal is approved, the WGS rates of grant are:

Area in hectares	Conifers per ha	Broadleaves per ha
0.25–0.9	£1005	£1575
1.0 –2.9	880	1375
3.0 –9.9	795	1175
10 and over	616	975

Where new planting is done on existing arable land or improved grassland which has been cultivated and reseeded within the last ten years, a 'better land supplement' of £400 and £600 per ha for conifers and broadleaves respectively is payable with the first instalment of the grant (see 5 below).

The terms of the grants have to be observed carefully; the salient points of the WGS are as follows:

1. Owners or tenants may apply for grants, provided that all the parties concerned in a particular land holding are joined in the application.

2. The minimum individual area eligible for grant is 0.25 ha. The grant band is fixed by the total of the areas approved for planting or regeneration in each separate wood within the five year period of the plan of operations.
3. Although an area for planting may generally be of any shape, it should harmonise with the landscape; very narrow strips are not encouraged on the grounds that they are difficult to manage either for timber production or amenity, and should better be funded as hedgerows or shelterbelts by an Agriculture Department (i.e. Ministry of Agriculture, Fisheries and Food, the Welsh Office Department of Agriculture or the Scottish Office Agriculture and Fisheries Department, MAFF, WOAD and SOAFD respectively).
4. Grants are payable for new planting, replanting or natural regeneration at the rates shown above. In all cases the suitability of the species is subject to the approval of the Forestry Commission. The rate of grant payable for mixtures is in proportion to the area occupied by conifers and approved broadleaves respectively; provided that the planting distances are uniform this means that the 'mixed' grant may be fixed by the proportions of the numbers of the two types of tree. For instance a mixture of one-third conifers and two-thirds broadleaves for a 1.0 ha planting would be:

$$(\frac{1}{3} \times 880) + (\frac{2}{3} \times 1375) = £1210$$

5. For new planting and replanting the grant is paid in three instalments, 70 per cent on completion of planting, 20 per cent after five years and 10 per cent after a further five years, subject to satisfactory establishment and maintenance. For natural regeneration the three instalments are 50 per cent, 30 per cent and 20 per cent, the first being paid on completion of the approved work which is designed to promote the natural seeding (this usually involves a heavy thinning or 'seeding felling', clearance of unwanted parent trees, clearing of weeds and perhaps soil cultivation). The second instalment is paid when an adequate stocking or desired species has been achieved and the third five years later, again subject to satisfactory maintenance.

EARLIER SCHEMES: TRANSITIONAL ARRANGEMENTS

Before the introduction of the Woodland Grant Scheme in April 1988, the Forestry Commission operated two other grant schemes to encourage the creation and management of woodlands: the Forestry Grant Scheme (FGS) and the Broadleaved Woodland Grant Scheme

(BWGS). These were closed to new applications from March 1988 but subsequent work done in accordance with existing approved plans of operations under FGS and BWGS continue to be eligible for the grants of those schemes. They also continue to be eligible until 1993 for Schedule D tax relief in respect of approved expenditure on those woods, even though woodland tax relief has been otherwise cancelled (see page 109).

The Farm Woodland Scheme (FWS)

This promotional scheme is designed specifically to encourage the establishment of new woodland on farms. It was introduced in October 1988, initially for a three year trial period, and is run jointly by the Forestry Commission and the Agriculture Departments (MAFF, WOAD & SOAFD). It offers both capital grants and annual payments at different rates and for a range of periods depending on the land planted and the species of trees used. The scheme is intended to appeal more to farmers of arable and improved grass than to upland and hill farmers; this is part of the national land use strategy of bringing afforestation 'down the hill', away from the uplands where it has been seen to be in sharpest conflict with nature conservation interests. Nevertheless, in order to accommodate hill farmers, sufficient funds have been allocated to afforest 3000 hectares of unimproved grazings in Less Favoured Areas (LFAs) over the period October 1988 to September 1991.

Approved tree planting under the FWS receives a Forestry Commission planting grant as follows:

Area in hectares	Conifers per ha	Broadleaves per ha
1.0–2.9	£505	£1375
3.0–9.9	420	1175
10 and over	240	975

The annual payments made by the Agriculture Departments are as follows:

(a) Arable land and grassland improved within the last ten years
  (i) Non-LFA — £190 per ha per annum
  (ii) LFA (Disadvantaged Areas) — £150 per ha per annum
  (iii) LFA (Severely Disadvantages Areas) — £100 per ha per annum

(b) Unimproved land in LFAs (DA and SDA) £30 per ha per annum

These annual payments will be made over 40 years for planting that is predominantly oak and beech; over 30 years for other broadleaves and mixed woodland comprising more than 50 per cent broadleaves by area; over 20 years for other woodland (i.e. more than 50 per cent conifer); and over 10 years for traditional coppice. The first payment is made the year after planting.

The following points are relevant to the FWS:

1. As in the WGS, tenants may apply provided they have the landlord's agreement.
2. The minimum size of each block to be planted is 1.0 hectare. The minimum area per holding to be planted in the three years of the initial scheme is 3.0 ha. The maximum area to be planted per holding is 40 hectares.
3. The expectations in respect of shape and design are similar to those of the WGS (point 3 on page 101); the pattern of existing field boundaries may be expected to exert special influence if excessive fencing costs are to be avoided.
4. The planting grants are paid by the Forestry Commission in three instalments: 70 per cent on completion of the planting, then 20 per cent and 10 per cent at five-yearly intervals thereafter, subject to satisfactory establishment and maintenance. The rate of grant payable for mixtures is in proportion to the area occupied by conifers and broadleaves, (as in the WGS, point 4 on page 101). The planting proposals have first to be accepted by the Forestry Commission which applies the same rules as in the WGS. Application forms are obtained from the local Forestry Commission Conservancy office.
5. The Forestry Commission planting grant is a capital grant and is tax-free. The annual payments made by the Agriculture Departments are taxable (see below).
6. The expectation is that the rates of grants will be reviewed in 1991 and thereafter at intervals of not more than 5 years.

SET-ASIDE SCHEME WOODLAND OPTIONS

Set-Aside is a voluntary scheme intended to induce farmers to take land out of food production and thereby to reduce the European Community's surplus capacity in certain arable crops. In return for taking out of production at least 20 per cent of their land growing certain arable crops (measured in the base year 1987/88) farmers receive annual payments of up to £200 per hectare.

There are two options for those farmers who wish to plant trees on Set-Aside land:

Option 1   Direct Set-Aside to Farm Woodland.

The Forestry Commission pays the grants of the Woodland Grant Scheme, on the terms set out on page 100, and the appropriate Agriculture Department pays amounts for the duration of the Set-Aside agreement (maximum 5 years):

| In LFAs | £180 per ha per annum for 5 years |
| Elsewhere | £200 per ha per annum for 5 years. |

Option 2   Set-Aside through the Farm Woodland Scheme.

The farmer who takes this option receives the planting grants and annual payments of the Farm Woodland Scheme as shown above and all the terms of the scheme apply (the duration of payments according to the tree species planted etc.). The area planted with trees can be counted towards the 20 per cent set-aside, which may be an advantage in deciding the whole farm strategy. Farmers who wish to plant more than the 40 ha limit allowed in the Farm Woodland Scheme may plant the balance under Option 1, Direct Set-Aside to Woodland, which provides the grant terms of the Woodland Grant Scheme.

Options 1 and 2 are not available for the establishment of fruit orchards, tree nurseries, Christmas trees or very short rotation coppice (e.g. 3 to 6 years) for bio-mass production.

MANAGEMENT GRANTS

In July 1990 the Forestry Commission announced proposals for additional grants to encourage better woodland management. The following paragraphs are taken from the Secretary of State for Scotland's response to a question in the House of Commons.

To qualify for the new grants, woodland owners will be required to agree to a five-year plan of operations with the Forestry Commission which will set out the management objectives and prescribe operations to advance those objectives during the period of the plan. The grants will be paid annually in arrears subject to satisfactory implementation of the plan. A lump sum payment of £100 will also be available from the Forestry Commission for owners who draw up management plans for the first time with the benefit of professional advice. (This assistance will not be available, however, for planting plans.) There will be two types of woodland management grant.

Standard management grants will be payable during the normal maintenance period following the initial establishment phase of the woodland—for conifer woodlands between 11 and 20 years of age and for broadleaved woodlands between 11 and 40 years. In return for these grants, owners will be obliged not only to carry out normal silvicultural operations to a high standard but also to take such steps as may be agreed between them and the Forestry Commission to increase the environmental value of the woodlands;

Special management grants will be payable for woodlands of special environmental value of any age above 10 years. In return for these grants, the owner will be required to agree to take specified action which will maintain and enhance the woodland's special character. Woodlands in this category will be those which in the Forestry Commission's view are of special value for nature conservation, landscape, public recreation or a combination of these by virtue of their nature, location or use. There will be a presumption that conifer and broadleaved woodlands properly classified as ancient and semi-natural in the inventory being drawn up by the Nature Conservancy Council will qualify, as will those of special landscape value in National Parks, Areas of Outstanding Natural Beauty, National Scenic Areas and those covered by woodland Tree Preservation Orders (TPOs). Each case, however, will have to be considered on its merits. Any woodland may qualify if the owner has proposals to establish, develop or improve free facilities for public access or for public recreation, provided the proposed facilities are in keeping with public demand and are accepted by the Forestry Commission. Owners in receipt of this special management grant will not be eligible to claim the standard management grant in respect of the same area.

A *supplementary grant* will be paid for woodlands of less than 10 hectares in either of the above categories in recognition of the higher management costs involved.

Subject to clearance by the European Commission under the terms of Article 93 of the Treaty of Rome, this significant extension to the Woodland Grant Scheme will come into operation on 1 April 1992, with the first grants being paid in 1993–94. The rates of woodland management grant and their periods of eligibility are given in Table 7.2. Woodland which is currently in receipt of grants from other public bodies will not be eligible for the woodland management grant, except for those woodlands established under the Farm Woodland Scheme. The annual payments to farmers under that scheme are compensation for agricultural income foregone, and are not provided for the purpose of defraying maintenance expenditure. Traditional coppice rotations will be eligible for management grants (in addition to the planting grant) whereas short rotation coppice will only be eligible for the planting grant.

Table 7.2   Woodland management grant rates effective from 1 April 1992

Type of grant	Period of eligibility (age of wood in years)	Rate of grant (£ per ha per annum)
Standard management grant		
Conifer	11–20	10
Broadleaved	11–40	25
Special management grant	11 onwards	35
Supplement for small woods		
Standard: Conifer	(as for main grant)	5
Broadleaved	(as for main grant)	10
Special grant	(as for main grant)	10

Note: Mixed woodlands will be eligible for the broadleaved and conifer element of the grant in proportion to the area occupied by the two categories: the rates of grant are those proposed in July 1990.

Shelterbelts and Hedgerows

Grants are available from the Agriculture Departments (MAFF, WOAD and SOAFD) to assist in the planting or restoration of shelterbelts and hedgerows. In the LFAs the rate is 60 per cent of approved costs, in the Crofting Counties 85 per cent. Elsewhere the rate is 30 per cent for hedges, hedgerow trees and shelterbelts which contain at least 50 per cent of broadleaved species; for belts which are mainly conifers the rate is 15 per cent of approved costs.

Amenity Planting and Wildlife Habitat

The Countryside Commission for Scotland and the Countryside Commission in England and Wales provide grants for the planting and management of amenity woodlands of up to a quarter hectare. The grants may be up to half the total expenditure but do not normally exceed that amount. In England and Wales the Countryside Commission is applying these funds especially, but not exclusively, to Community forests on the fringes of some cities.

    Similarly the Nature Conservancy Council may give grants up to 50 per cent of costs for planting and management of small woods where the primary objective is nature conservation and the provision of wildlife habitat.

The National Park authorities in England and Wales may provide financial aid to owners or tenants in National Parks only, for key amenity tree planting and small scale woodland management, especially for work which does not qualify for aid from other sources. Application should be made to the National Park Officer. Similarly the Tree Council may give grants up to 50 per cent of costs for approved tree and woodland projects aimed at amenity and conservation outside National Park areas.

Environmentally Sensitive Areas (ESAs)

These schemes are in the control of the Agriculture Departments and trees feature in only some of them. ESAs are farming areas which have some outstanding ecological features which, it is intended, should be conserved. The objectives and mechanisms of each ESA scheme are unique and payments vary. Payments are made only to farmers in return for agreement to follow specified prescriptions (for instance, excluding sheep from a defined piece of woodland) and the amounts are set by the Departments individually for each Area. Farmers who enter ESA agreements may also use other schemes, such as the FWS above, provided they do not receive duplicate financial help for the same work and that the planting proposals do not conflict with the ESA objectives. (See Chapter 6).

General Woodland Strategy

In recent years the Forestry Commission has placed special emphasis on the conservation of broadleaved woodland, that is to say of trees such as oak, beech, ash and sycamore, and this is well reflected in the structure of the main tree planting grants with their obvious differentials between the rates paid for broadleaves and conifers. The principles of the official policy are as follows:

- Woodland which is now broadleaved is expected to remain so, which means that areas felled in broadleaved woods should be replaced either directly with broadleaves or with planting which will develop effectively into broadleaved woodland.

- There is a presumption against clearance of broadleaved woodland for agricultural purposes, and very strong reasons would have to be put forward for this to be allowed.

- Special attention is given to 'ancient semi-natural' broadleaved wood-lands (see page 8) to ensure that their special features are maintained; these woods are virtually irreplaceable and their special, natural characteristics must not be lost.

- The present area of broadleaved woodland is expected to increase by new broadleaved planting on what is now farm land, by the natural colonisation of broadleaved trees on open or waste land, and by some planting of broadleaved species to replace conifers.

- Managed woodland is more likely to survive than unmanaged woodland. With proper management an income can be obtained from the woods without harm to landscape, wildlife conservation or recreation interests, all of which can be met better by healthy, valuable trees than by moribund ones.

The grants available for planting broadleaves are substantially higher than those payable for conifers or mixed species. The farmer, how-ever, should remember that broadleaved trees, when grown in the tra-ditional way, generally take substantially longer than conifers to reach maturity or marketable size, and the costs of establishment are usually considerably higher. To some extent at least, these differences are reflected in the rates of grants offered by the Forestry Commission.

If, in the opinion of the Forestry Commission, planting has not been done properly or maintained to a good standard, grants may be with-held or recovered with interest. In the event of a farm sale, the seller should consider the need for an indemnity if any grant instalments are outstanding since the burden of repayment would fall on the person who received the original grant, not on the subsequent occupier who might be responsible for the neglect.

Both within the Agriculture Departments in Britain and in the European Commission a revision of the Common Agricultural Policy has been promoted whereby farmers are being encouraged to plant trees on land which has hitherto been in food production. The prin-cipal hindrance to this change of land use is obviously the farmer's expectation that he would suffer a loss of income through the non-productive years between tree planting and wood harvest; he would lose his income from food crops through that whole period. That loss would extend perhaps to twenty years in the most productive conifer-ous plantations in traditional management, about thirty-five years on slower-growing conifers and around fifty years on traditionally man-aged broadleaved woodland. These estimates are probably realistic in past traditional forest management. In some instances the farmer may be able to reduce those periods by innovative and intensive management, for instance by growing Christmas trees or by harvesting stakes from the coniferous 'nurses' in broadleaved planting, or in some areas from the sale of young broadleaved thinnings for firewood, for which a brisk demand has recently arisen in some areas. It must be recognised, however, that in some cases he would be unable to obtain this type of income and might well be constrained in such management by conservation pressures. The Farm Woodland Scheme, offering both capital grant for planting and annual grant income over an extended period, is the British government's response, as also is the Set-Aside directly to woodland.

Although the rules of the Farm Woodland Scheme and the Woodland Grant Scheme are being reconsidered to provide financial support for very short rotation crops for biomass (say 3 to 5 years), farmers should also consider carefully the possibilities on fertile ground of raising quick-growing broadleaved crops on slightly longer rotations. *On suitable sites* some cultivars of poplar will mature in 12 to 20 years and on others alders such as *Alnus rubra* may mature in similar periods and could be cut as coppice to provide material that can be sold for chipboard manufacture. Special conditions must be met:

- Only disease resistant clones of poplar hybrids may be used, by regulation.

- There must be a market for the produce such as pulp or chipboard—check with the local Forestry Commission office.

- The more specialised the crop, the stronger the case for the farmer to obtain specialist advice on the species, the appropriate clone or cultivar and the suitability of the site.

The short production period of these broadleaved crops, coupled with the high planting grants and the availability of annual payments, may make their cultivation much more attractive financially than might be supposed from the traditional opinions on broadleaved tree planting.

TAXATION

The Finance Act of 1988 create major changes for forest management in respect of income taxation. Previously the forest owner had the alternatives of being assessed under Schedule B or Schedule D, which offered the choice of either a sustained tax payment on a low assumed income irrespective of actual profit, or of offsetting the high afforestation investment cost against other taxable income (an opportunity especially attractive to high income tax payers). In effect the 1988 budget took forestry entirely out of the income tax system.

At the time of writing there has been insufficient opportunity to test the new situation and gauge the full implications of the change. The large forestry investor is no longer able to set afforestation costs or other net forestry losses against other sources of taxable income, and in consequence the rate of upland afforestation has slowed dramatically since the tax change. Although this was the obvious and immediate result, the effects are more far-reaching: the planting grant payments to farmers (Woodland Grant Scheme and Farm Woodland Scheme grants) are not subject to income tax, nor are timber receipts in a forestry enterprise.

It should be noted, however, that the annual income received from Agriculture Departments under the Farm Woodland Scheme and the various Set-Aside options is taxable, as are receipts from game shooting in woodland, Christmas tree sales etc.

In this considerable area of doubt concerning liability, farmers should probably seek the advice of their usual tax or financial adviser or the services of a professional forestry consultant. The position is clear for the commercial forestry enterprise which is directed to growing timber, but is less clear for a farmer whose trees are not primarily for timber production but intended, say, for shelter. The growing of such trees may be regarded as strictly ancillary to the farming activity, chargeable to the farm account and therefore assessable under the usual Schedule D for the farm, both in respect of maintenance costs and income from certain grants or incidental sales. Between these two extremes there will be a transition from untaxable to fully taxable, which will be subject to judgment and precedent. A farmer who intends to invest substantially in woodland, whether with his own labour or with contractors, should take professional accountancy advice about the tax position in order to obtain the maximum advantage.

Standing timber is not subject to Capital Gains Tax, even though the growth of the tree from seedling to maturity is essentially an example of capital growth. Cut timber, however, is subject to Capital Gains Tax, although the situation will rarely arise in the farming situation.

Woodland capital is treated in a broadly similar fashion to other farm capital in respect of Inheritance Tax. It seems unlikely that consideration of liability to Inheritance Tax would be critical in a farmer's decision to manage or create woodland on a farm scale. In most situations the total tax liability might be marginally reduced by

a farmer engaging in forestry, seldom increased, but where a propor-
tionately large scale transfer of land and capital into forestry is being
contemplated, specialist advice should be obtained. Each instance is
probably unique.

Conservation

In earlier chapters the reader has been reminded of the need to ensure
that new woodlands enhance the farm's value for wildlife as well as its
productive and income earning capacity. Some aspects of conservation
are protected by the law and the farmer should be aware of them.

The key modern legislation in this regard is the Wildlife and
Countryside Act 1981, a long and very wide-ranging statute which can
bear on almost every activity in country life. It empowers the Nature
Conservancy Council (NCC) to designate Sites of Special Scientific
Interest (SSSIs)—areas which are considered to have features of high
value for conservation. Neither ownership nor tenancy is directly
affected by SSSI designation but the intention is that the occupier of
the land should not operate in any way which would destroy or damage
the special feature that has been noted.

The feature of the SSSI might be an ancient monument such as
an old road or ditch system which would be destroyed by forestry
ploughing, or it might be a special plant community which would
be sensitive to herbicide application or to the deep shade of conifer
planting. Whatever is intended to be conserved, the NCC has a duty
to tell the landowner, in writing, the boundary of an SSSI and which
operations would affect the site. The landholder on his part must give
notice to the NCC if he intends to carry out any of the 'potentially
damaging' operations listed in the SSSI notification, in sufficient time
for them to discuss the matter and take action if they wish. Many kinds
of quite normal work like draining, fertilising and tree planting could
cause serious changes in the conservation area, so the farmer should
check the papers relating to an SSSI on his land carefully before
starting any woodland work. Full discussions should be held with the
NCC Regional Officer well in advance of any work contemplated in
an SSSI.

If the operation of an SSSI notification causes the farmer financial
loss by restricting his normal management of the land, he should claim
financial reimbursement from the NCC. It may be appropriate for him
to take skilled advice on such a claim if he has not had earlier experience since the matter is an unusual one. Since mid-1989, however,

compensation has not been payable in respect of loss of income arising from refusal of clearance to plant and consequent withholding of planting grant, where the refusal is solely on grounds of native conservation.

The Wildlife and Countryside Act also seeks to conserve the variety of plants and animals by controlling their disturbance, killing and removal. It is the farmer's responsibility to be aware of this and to ensure that plants and animals are not unnecessarily adversely affected by farming activities. The protected birds are listed in Schedule 1 of the Act, other animals in Schedule 5 and plants in Schedule 8. The NCC Regional Officers have copies of the Act and its Schedules, and so also should local libraries.

It sometimes happens that a protected animal is killed or a protected plant is destroyed in the course of quite normal and lawful operations, losses which could not reasonably have been prevented: an animal killed under the tractor wheels or rare plants eaten by a cow. It is a defence in law that such destruction does not constitute an offence since it was incidental to a lawful operation. Nevertheless clear legal guidelines have not yet been laid down by court decisions for what can, or can not, be reasonably avoided. The farmer should be especially careful in the proper handling of powerful herbicides and pesticides (and in the disposal of 'empty' containers), and should inform himself fully of the law before setting some kinds of traps in woodland areas, or allowing other people to set them on his land, since penalties on conviction could be severe.

Well-planned and well-managed farm woods should enhance wild-life values in the countryside and should not bring the owner into any conflict with the conservation law. The local FWAG (or FFWAG) officer is likely to be a very useful contact in this respect (see page 139). The farmer who has an SSSI designated on his land should aim to have a constructive relationship with the local Regional Officer of the NCC, rather then a defensive one.

Safety

Farmers are likely to be well versed in their responsibilities in respect of the Health and Safety at Work legislation. Needless to say it applies to woodlands as much as to the rest of the farm. Special attention is drawn to a few salient points:

- The common chain saw is highly dangerous in untrained hands.

- Several useful woodland machines work from the power take-off of the tractor: guard it—it is far more dangerous when people are working at the back of the tractor than it is with the driver in his cab.

- A circular saw without its top guard and riving knife is vicious: it should never be so operated, no matter how strong the temptation for convenience.

- A falling tree, or one caught up in its neighbours' branches, contains awesome power to crush a person when it falls, even if it is of modest size. As a tree lands, the butt can jump, or whip back, and when a workman who thinks it is safely on the ground is simply trimming off the branches, the tree can roll over if these happen to be holding it up.

Competent contractors working in a farmer's woods nowadays should know how to go about jobs safely; the farmer should be aware whether or not legal responsibility for accidents to employees and contractors who are using unsafe practices rests with the owner of the property. A comprehensive set of free leaflets is produced by the Forestry Safety Council (address in Appendix 3).

Particular note should be made of recent legislation regarding the safe use of chemicals on the land and their storage or disposal, embodied in the Food and Environment Protection Act, 1985 (FEPA), the Control of Pesticide Regulations, 1986 and the Control of Substances Hazardous to Health Act, 1988 (COSHH). A certificate of competence is *required* for the use of specified chemicals on someone else's land and is, of course, *recommended* for the use on one's own land. Certificates can be obtained by successfully completing approved FEPA training courses which are held by the Agricultural Training Board and some agricultural colleges, including the Scottish Agricultural College.

Timber Felling

The intention of various Forestry Acts has been to give the Forestry Commission, as the national Forest Authority, powers to prevent woodland being destroyed. The Commission controls the felling of trees throughout Great Britain and requires that the owners of woodland obtain a felling licence before the work is done. There are legal exceptions to this rule where:

- the felling is in accordance with an approved plan of operations under one of the Forestry Commission's grant schemes;

- the trees are in a garden, orchard, churchyard or public open space;

- the trees are all below 8 centimetres in diameter, measured 1.3 metres from the ground; or in the case of thinnings, below 10 centimetres in diameter; or in the case of coppice or underwood, below 15 centimetres;

- the trees are interfering with permitted development or statutory works by public bodies;

- the trees are dead, dangerous, causing a nuisance or are badly affected by Dutch Elm Disease.

In addition to these exceptions, an owner of woodland may cut a total of 5 cubic metres, and sell up to 2 cubic metres of that amount, in any three month period.

Applications for a felling licence should be made to the local Forestry Commission office: a map of the property showing the location of the site is required, together with the number of trees, their species and estimated volume. Updated information can be found in the Forestry Commission's free leaflet 'Control of Tree Felling' available from all Forestry Commission offices.

The farmer who has a clear plan of management for his woods should encounter no difficulty in receiving the licence. It will normally stipulate as a condition that the area to be cleared should be promptly and effectively regenerated. As has been already described, broad-leaved woodland will be expected to be replaced with broadleaves, and mixed broadleaved and conifer woodland similarly. The proper replanting in a reasonable time is a legal responsibility. Replanting or natural regeneration usually qualifies for a grant under the Woodland Grant Scheme (see Table 7.1 and page 100).

Tree Preservation Orders

A farmer may find that some of his trees have been subject to Tree Preservation Orders (TPOs). These orders are made under the Town and Country Planning (Tree Preservation Order) Regulations and a landowner whose trees are subject to a TPO must be so informed by the Council making the order. The trees must also be identified clearly on a suitable map. Similarly the seller of land is bound to notify a buyer that a TPO has been made in respect of trees on the property.

A planning committee's intention in imposing a TPO is to conserve the tree and protect amenity, and the order may indeed achieve that for some time, perhaps for several years. Nevertheless an order imposed on an area of woodland for many years may have the opposite effect by leaving the trees to die of old age and neglect and failing to provide for their replacement, a point now well understood by most Planning Officers.

A farmer with a TPO on his woodlands who intends to sustain them by responsible management should get in touch with the Planning Officer of the Council which imposed the TPO with a view to lifting the order when it is necessary to allow appropriate management. The agreed practice has been for woodlands being managed under the Dedication Scheme to be exempt from TPOs and it is in line with that agreement that a Planning Officer should vary or lift the order if he is convinced that the owner plans to conserve the woodland, and thereby promote the order's long-term intention.

Certainly the imposition of a TPO may seriously reduce the value of woodland property and an owner is well advised to discuss the position with the Planning Officers in order to understand their real concerns and intentions. Evidence of a proper scheme of responsible management, involving appropriate replacement and enhancement of the woodlands, may well be effective in lifting the restrictions and allowing good management to be exercised.

If the proposed felling of trees covered by a TPO comes within one of the exceptions from felling licensing listed above, an application for consent to fell should be made directly to the planning authority. If, however, the proposed felling would also require a licence, an application should be made in the first instance to the Forestry Commission who will forward it, with their comments, to the planning authority.

The most sensitive issues in TPOs are usually very old prominent trees which are landmarks well known by the public. The question of legal responsibility for their retention into senility may arise. The parties may have to face the payment of heavy premiums to provide special public liability insurance to indemnify the farmer against claims for damage inflicted by a tree which he wanted to remove before it became unsafe but which he was denied permission to fell.

Unsafe Trees

It may happen that a tree which was apparently quite healthy and stable falls without warning or is blown down in a severe storm, doing damage to people and property. The owner of the tree would not be held responsible in law for the damage if the failure of the tree could not reasonably have been foreseen or prevented. On the other hand, if the tree had obvious signs of weakness or ill health, the owner might expect to be held financially responsible for the damage caused by his dangerous property—the tree—and to be successfully sued.

The damages which might arise from a defective tree falling across a farm boundary, say onto a public road and causing a traffic accident, could be enormous. Consequently there is every good reason for the farmer to look carefully at all trees along boundaries and within falling distance of public paths and places where people may be expected. There is no need for highly specialised knowledge in making the regular inspection. It is the sharp eye of a commonly sensible person that a court would expect to be used in deciding what could reasonably have been foreseen. Look out for:

—leaning trees;
—trees with roots that heave up in a breeze;
—trees with large dead branches and unhealthy crowns;
—trees with bracket fungi growing from the bole;
—trees with toadstools growing round them;
—trees that are hollow or have pockets of rot.

If the farmer himself is uncertain about the safety of a tree he should get an outside opinion from a local forester or forestry consultant. The farm adviser or the local Forestry Commission office would suggest someone suitable. (A leaflet describing external signs of decay in trees is referred to in Appendix 2.)

Well-tended woods formed of suitable species and managed so that the trees are harvested at normal maturity seldom give anxiety or trouble. Neglected, unhealthy trees left to waste into senility are usually the dangerous ones.

Planting Clearance

Although not part of the law, it is appropriate to refer here to the practice of obtaining clearance for afforestation proposals.

The environmental impact of large afforestation schemes is so great that the Forestry Commission informs certain statutory bodies, and some non-statutory, about new planting proposals and discusses their details with a view to agreeing or 'clearing' schemes which should not damage sensitive environments. The application for planting clearance arises when the planting qualifies for grant aid under one of the forestry grant schemes. The Forestry Commission normally refers applications to all the bodies likely to have interests directly affected: agriculture, water authorities, local authorities for amenity, nature conservation, the Red Deer Commission in the Scottish Highlands and so on. If objections raised cannot be resolved by discussion among the officers concerned, the application may be referred to the Forestry Commission's Regional Advisory Committee (RAC) which meets periodically to handle such problems. The RACs are composed mainly of people with farming, forestry and land agency experience. Particularly intractable disputes may be referred to the Forestry Minister concerned for decision (the Minister of Agriculture in England, the Secretary of State for Scotland and the Secretary of State for Wales). Such contentious cases are likely to be the large forestry schemes. Farm woodlands are usually much less controversial.

In some Regions of Scotland the process of obtaining clearance for planting has been revised recently, with the development of 'Indicative Forestry Strategies'. The initial work on this type of strategy was done in Strathclyde Region. The strategy is based on site and soil surveys, interpreted by groups of scientists and planners, including those concerned with farming, nature conservation and landscape conservation, as well as foresters. The outcome is a map published by the Regional Council, which identifies areas where afforestation would be regarded generally as intrusive and unwelcome, areas where special care would be required in the design of new planting and areas where further afforestation could be accepted subject to the usual consultation conditions. The new indicative strategies are intended to avoid the submission of applications for planting clearance in areas unsuitable for afforestation, which would be directly opposed and most likely to fail. They are seen as part of the greater sensitivity in respect of land use change and the recent moves towards much closer attention to design in forestry planning and landscaping.

It should be noted that, under EEC regulations, any afforestation project may now be required to have an Environmental Assessment prepared if it would have a significant impact on the environment. This does apply to large planting schemes and could apply to some farm woods though it is unlikely they would be large enough to require one. A similar position exists in relation to the impact of afforestation on drainage and water catchment; planting grant applications will be referred to the water authority if necessary.

Neighbours

Among the common contentious matters involving trees, reference must be made to nuisance arising from trees on boundaries. These may cause problems by shading, dripping or sending roots into the neighbour's land.

In law a landowner has no right to the light and air space and root space in the earth beyond the boundary line of his property. In the event of a boundary dispute concerning trees a reasonable sequence of events to reduce the nuisance might be as follows.

The person suffering nuisance should specify it (loss of light, drip, roots invading tile drains, etc.) and ask the owner of the trees to act to reduce it. The owner of the tree may then cut the branches or the roots involved, or he may ask the neighbour to cut them.

If the owner of the tree does not act in reasonable time to put the matter right, the neighbour suffering the trouble may take action himself. He should give notice that he intends to cut the offending branches, etc., and he must take care to avoid damaging the trees beyond the boundary, since they are not his property. He may cut branches or roots only where they cross the boundary, working on his own property, and, in addition to abating the nuisance, he may sue for damages if actual damage has been caused.

The owner of woodland has particular responsibilities in law to neighbours in respect of water. The cultivation of land for forestry planting or the application of fertiliser or herbicides must be done in such a way that it does not damage water rights or fisheries and angling. To this end forestry ploughing should be designed so that furrows stop well short of streams, and drainage ditches should have a gradient of only about two degrees in order to minimise soil washing into streams; the danger is that fine soil is carried to the areas where fish breed, usually banks of clean gravel, where it kills the eggs or young fish and prevents subsequent breeding. Similarly, it is important that timber working should be conducted so that soil and felling debris from the trees do not enter streams; the worst danger is usually from soil washing into streams from roads made muddy by tyres.

Reference for Further Reading

See Appendix 2.

Chapter 8

THE WOODLAND HARVEST

THE WOODLAND harvest takes place periodically throughout the life of a tree crop, normally every five to ten years. Trees are cut for two main reasons—to relieve competition (thinning) and to allow regeneration, either artificial (planting) or natural, as discussed in Chapters 2 and 4. In even-aged stands thinning is carried out during the latter half to two-thirds of the rotation and the whole stand is clearfelled and replanted at rotation age. In uneven-aged stands individual trees or groups of trees are felled to allow regeneration at the same time as the rest of the crop is thinned.

The most important questions to ask are 'how much can be harvested?' and 'what return can be expected?' The answer to the second question depends on the type of material harvested, how this is marketed and who does the work. But first consideration will be given to the quantity of timber to be expected.

TIMBER YIELD

Timber yield depends on site conditions and tree species, and is estimated by a site index called Yield Class (YC).

Figure 8.1 shows how tree crops grow over time. Each year the trees increase in size and the total increase—expressed in cubic metres per hectare—is called the Current Annual Increment (CAI). Values of CAI range up to about 20 m^3/ha/yr for pines, larches and broadleaves, and up to twice this value for spruces, true firs (*Abies*) and Douglas fir. Since 1 cubic metre of green timber weighs approximately 1 tonne this increment can be compared with annual yields of root crops or cereals expressed in tonnes per hectare.

CAI increases rapidly to a maximum value at about half the rotation age and then falls, more gradually, as tree growth decreases in old age. The Mean Annual Increment (MAI) is the *average* yield up to any

119

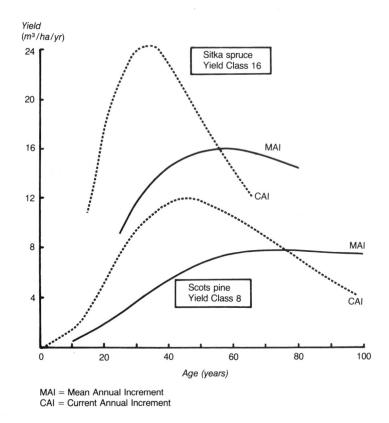

Figure 8.1   Growth of tree crops over time.

particular age. The MAI curve climbs more slowly to a maximum value and stays much the same over a period of ten to twenty years before declining slowly.

The MAI has two main uses. Firstly, the age of maximum MAI is the obvious time to fell an even-aged plantation if timber yield is the primary objective; in other words, it is a good first estimate of rotation length. Secondly, maximum MAI defines the site index 'Yield Class' (check this on Figure 8.1) which states how much yield can be expected from a given species on a particular site in the long term. This is best illustrated by a number of examples:

1. *Total Production = MAI (to date) × Age*
   e.g. Scots pine, YC 8, age 50.
      From Figure 8.1, MAI at age 50 = 7 m³/ha/yr (approx.).
      Total production to date = 7 × 50 = 350 m³/ha.

2. *Annual Thinning Yield = 70% Yield Class*
   e.g. Sitka spruce, YC 16.
   Annual thinning yield = $0.7 \times 16 = 11.2$ m³/ha/yr.
   Therefore, if we thin this crop every five years we could expect to harvest (5×11.2) or 56 m³/ha from fully stocked stands, once thinning has started in the second half of the rotation. The age of first thinning varies with species and Yield Class, as shown in Table 8.1.

3. *Standing Volume = Total Production – Total Thinnings*
   A useful rule of thumb for even-aged stands is that over a whole rotation thinnings represent about half of the *total* production, the other half being felled at rotation age.

4. *Sustained Annual Yield = Yield Class* × Area
   If a wood contains approximately equal areas of each age class of trees up to the rotation age its yield is simply (YC × Area) m³ per annum in perpetuity.
   For example, Sitka spruce YC 16; rotation = 55 years; area = 5.5 ha, made up of eleven stands, each occupying 0.5 ha, aged, 5, 10, 15 . . . 45, 50, 55.
   Sustained annual yield = $16 \times 5.5 = 88$ m³/year.
   In practice the stands aged between 20 and 50 would be thinned every five years and each stand would be felled when it reached the age of 55. Together (thinnings and clearfelling) the periodic yield would be $5 \times 88 = 440$ m³ every five years.

If a wood contains trees of only one age or a limited range of ages periodic yields will fluctuate over time, although the cumulative total over the whole rotation will be the same as if a balanced age structure existed (Figure 8.2). It is therefore desirable to aim for a balanced area distribution of age classes if regular production is required. This can be achieved either by having a number of even-aged stands as in the example above, which can be located in one block or in several woods around the farm, or by having uneven-aged woodland where each stand contains a balanced mixture of ages. The former is definitely easier to manage, though the latter may be more attractive and provide greater habitat diversity.

Tables of timber yield for different species and Yield Classes are published on separate A5 sheets as part of Forestry Commission Booklet No. 48. You also need to specify both initial spacing and type of thinning in order to choose the right 'yield model' to match your crop.

Finally, a word of caution! Yield Class is a site index indicating the

Table 8.1. Standard ages of first thinning (years)

Species (planted at 2 × 2 m)	Yield Class					
	22	18	14	10	6	4
oak, sweet chestnut					28	36
beech				26	32	35
ash, birch, cherry, sycamore				15	20	25
Scots, lodgepole pine			21	26	35	41
Corsican pine		20	22	27	36	
European larch				20	26	32
Japanese, hybrid larch			15	18	23	27
Douglas fir	17	19	22	27		
Norway spruce	21	23	26	31	41	
Sitka spruce	19	21	23	27	35	
Lawson cypress	22	24	28			

Adapted with kind permission of the Forestry Commission from *Thinning Control*, Field Book 2.

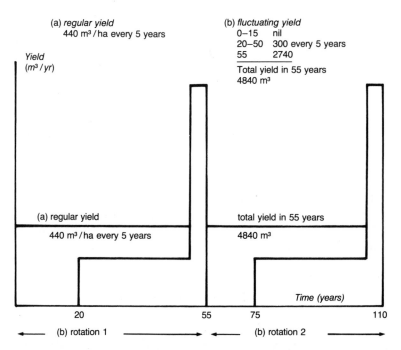

Figure 8.2   Yield from 5.5 ha of Sitka spruce, Yield Class 16: (a) eleven stands of 0.5 ha, aged 5, 10, 15 . . . 55; (b) one even-aged stand of 5.5 ha.

Table 8.2. Guide to normal woodland stocking

Average tree diameter (cm)	Spacing (m)	Normal stocking density (trees/ha)
less than 10 (i.e. newly planted or regenerated)	1.5–3	4000 – 1200
10–20	2.5–3.5	1700 – 800
20–30	4–6	600 – 300
30–40	5–7	400 – 200
40–50	6–8	300 – 150
50–60	8–10	150 – 100
greater than 65	10–14	100 – 50

Note:

1. Wider spacing means lower stocking, and vice versa:
   overstocking: trees are too close if the stocking density is greater than the above figures;
   understocking: trees are too few if the stocking density is less than the above figures.

2. The age at which a given average diameter is reached will depend on species and Yield Class.

3. The initial spacing for commercial tree crops is normally 2 metres; 1.5–2 m spacing involves more work and cost but may improve tree form, especially in broadleaves; 3 m spacing (normally in tree shelters) is the maximum accepted for the Woodland Grant Scheme.

Adapted with kind permission of ADAS and the Forestry Commission from *Practical Work in Farm Woods*.

potential for tree growth: *actual* production will also depend on management. Actual volume may be less than yield table predictions because of poor stocking, due to inadequate weeding or windblow for example, and Table 8.2 gives a guide to appropriate levels of stocking. In addition, yield tables give volumes *per hectare* and assume that the whole area is productive: a reduction of 15 per cent from the total area is normally made for roads and rides within the wood and further reductions may be necessary for unplanted land such as ponds or storage areas.

TIMBER VALUE

The return to be expected from harvesting small parcels of timber typical of farm woodlands is notoriously difficult to estimate precisely because of their variability. In order to determine the value of individual mature trees, or a potential thinning, an estimate needs to be made of the quantity to be felled and its unit value:

$$Timber\ value = \begin{array}{c} Timber\ Quantity \\ (m^3,\ tonnes) \end{array} \times \begin{array}{c} Unit\ Value \\ (\pounds/m^3,\ \pounds/tonne) \end{array}$$

The unit value will depend on a number of factors:

- the type and quality of material—size, species and condition;
- location of timber for sale—standing, felled ('at stump') or extracted to a lorry loading point ('at roadside');
- accessibility—gradient and ground conditions within the wood, quality of track or road and distance to a lorry loading point;
- the overall quantity—small quantities tend to raise unit costs;
- who does the work—farm labour, contractors;
- type of sale—negotiation, auction or tender.

Type of material required for different markets
The main markets, specifications, and approximate values for timber products are listed in Table 8.3a and illustrated in Plates 8.1–8.4.

Points to note are the general increase in unit value with size (diameter) and the wide range of value for different markets, particularly for hardwoods. In addition prices vary from month to month, year to year, and in different parts of the country. Inspection of the appropriate trade journals to consider the timber market before making a sale (see list of journals in Appendix 2) can be time well spent. Timber quality will also affect price, again particularly for hardwoods (Table 8.3b): the main features to aim for are straightness of stem and small branching, freedom from stain, splits and rot. Care in presenting timber for sale is increasingly cost-effective as the unit value increases. Quality timber can be used for any purpose but the reverse is not the case, and for most farm woodlands it will pay to grow the highest-quality timber that site conditions permit.

Location of the timber
The increase in value at successive stages in the harvesting process is illustrated in Figure 8.3. The unit costs of felling and extraction decrease with tree size, and extraction costs will also depend on distance to the road, ground conditions—and the weather! It usually pays to wait until

the ground is dry to minimise soil and root damage, not to mention unsightly ruts and the risk of getting bogged down. The choice of selling standing or at roadside will depend on the availability of machinery and manpower to carry out the harvesting operation. As a general rule less valuable material (e.g. early thinnings) can be sold standing but more valuable material (e.g. sports-quality ash) is best sold at stump or roadside where the buyer can inspect each stem closely. Early thinnings and 'run of the mill' conifer sawlogs are generally bought on a tonnage

Table 8.3a. Markets for timber products

Market or grade	Log diameter overbark (cm)	Length (m)	Species preferred	Value at roadside 1990 (£/tonne)
'Small roundwood'				
pulpwood			spruce	
fencing			larch, sweet chestnut	
mining	6–20	2–3	all (*except* poplar, willow)	15–20
firewood	(40)		hardwoods	
particle board			all (limit on larch)	
Conifer sawlogs	12–45			
(softwood)	(60)			
pallets, fencing		2–3	all	15–30
general construction		3+, tree	all	20–40
special markets				
e.g. boatskins		as	larch	50–70
telegraph poles		specified	pine, larch, D. fir	45–55
Broadleaf sawlogs				
(hardwood)				
low grade				
mining	25+	as	all (*except* poplar, willow)	15–30
pallet	30+	specified	all	
fencing	35+		oak	
planking quality	40+	2.5+	ash, oak, sweet chestnut	30–120
	25+		beech, sycamore	
veneer	40+	3+	ash, oak, sweet chestnut sycamore, cherry, walnut	up to 200
special markets	10+	short		up to 300
e.g. turnery		lengths	lime	
marquetry		can be valuable	apple, box laburnum	

Note: (i) *Standing values* will be £5–18 less than the *roadside values* (i.e. net of harvesting costs), with small diameter trees on sites with difficult access being the most expensive to harvest.
(ii) Brackets denote maximum sizes normally accepted.

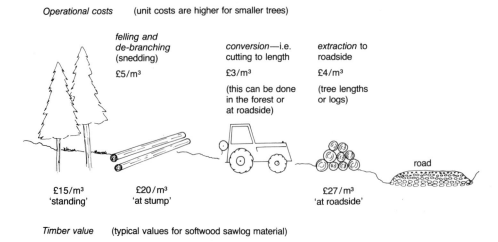

Figure 8.3　Timber value at different stages of harvesting.

basis, measured at a weighbridge, whereas high-value softwood and most hardwood logs are bought on the basis of individual tree volume. Note that recently felled timber weighs nearly 1 tonne/m³; seasoned (air-dried) timber weighs approximately half this amount.

Accessibility

This is of particular importance if timber production is a primary objective, though ease of access benefits all operations. Access should always be considered when planning to upgrade existing woodland or plant new areas, and in woods larger than about two hectares internal tracks or rides should be left as permanent extraction routes.

Both the quality of access to the wood and movement within the wood determine extraction costs and hence timber value. Do not forget that road capacity is limited by bridge width, or height, as well as strength!

Overall quantity

This has little bearing on felling costs but can increase the cost of extraction and haulage if the total quantity is less than 20 tonnes (one lorry load). It may be possible to combine operations with a neighbour and share haulage to overcome this problem.

Harvesting operations

Timber harvesting is a skilled operation, requiring training and experience to achieve the costs given in Figure 8.3. It includes felling,

Table 8.3b **Proportions of different quality grades in an average parcel of hardwood timber**

Species	Quality	Relative value	% volume	% value
Beech	mining/pallet	1	20	10
	planking	1½–2½	80	90
Ash	mining/pallet	1	25	10
	planking	1½–4	70	80
	veneer	5½	5	10
Oak	mining/pallet	1	15	5
	fencing	2	35	25
	planking	2½–6	45	45
	veneer	10	5	25

Adapted, with kind permission, from Henry Venables Ltd, Stafford.

Plate 8.1   Small roundwood: a roadside stack of 3 m hardwood pulp in S. Wales; the smaller material would be equally suitable for firewood.

Plate 8.2   Conifer sawlogs: fifty-year-old Scots pine, E. Anglia.

Plate 8.3 Broadleaf sawlogs: moderate-quality beech, age about a hundred years, in the Chilterns; note the bent and damaged log which can only be used for 'down-market' mining timber.

Plate 8.4 Veneer-quality oak butt, Staffordshire.

debranching (or 'snedding'), conversion (cutting to specified lengths) and extraction to a lorry loading point or a storage location on the farm (Plates 8.5–8.8). The cutting operations are carried out by chainsaw or remotely controlled cutting heads attached to specialised forestry harvesting equipment. Conversion may take place in the wood or at roadside, requiring extraction of either 'short wood' or tree lengths respectively. The former is done by a tractor-trailer combination, loaded hydraulically or by hand, and the latter by winch (ground-skidding) or a cable crane system if tractor access is difficult. More details of these operations and suitable machinery may be found in Forestry Commission Bulletin No. 14.

Small farm woods will not normally provide the quantity of work to justify investment in specialised equipment although the use of farm tractors may be appropriate, adapted by adding a suitable winch. Larger woodland areas may generate sufficient production work to justify the purchase of forestry harvesting equipment, in which case advice from specialist suppliers should always be sought. It will normally cost more for farmers to carry out their own harvesting operations, unless the quantity of work justifies the investment in suitable equipment and training. This means selling standing, or employing contractors to fell and extract to the roadside. The exception is likely to be early thinnings or coppice working in small blocks where the material (and total quantity) is small enough to be manhandled to the woodland edge. Horse extraction can be cost-effective if skilled handlers are available locally.

Harvesting operations are potentially dangerous and it is wise to take any necessary precautions and to follow safe working practices as described by the Forestry Safety Council (see page 112).

Type of sale
Timber can be sold by direct negotiation, auction or tender. While the first may be applicable for small quantities or specialised products, sale by tender has the advantage that the marketing is carried out by a specialist in that field. Offers should always be sought from at least two contractors or buyers to ensure that the real market price is obtained. It is not always best to accept the highest offer—one may prefer a slightly lower sum from a reliable operator who works carefully and pays promptly! A simple contract should be drafted for signature by both parties stating the quantity of timber concerned, the agreed price and when this is to be paid, and other local details such as repair to fences or roads as appropriate. A suitable format is given below. Do not forget that virtually all felling requires a licence, unless it is part of an agreed work programme under a Forestry Commission grant scheme (see page 113).

Suggested Considerations in a Contract for Standing Sale of Timber

1. Location
(a) Map (scale at least 1:10,000) with the boundary of the working area, and access from the public road, clearly marked.
(b) O.S. Grid Reference of a suitable point marked on the map.

2. Description of trees
(a) Species, and proportion, by volume, if more than one species.
(b) Estimated mean diameter (or mean volume) and total volume— for thinnings, and clear-fellings of average-quality timber.
or
  Diameter, condition, and estimated volume *per tree*—for small numbers of mature trees, and any fellings of high-quality timber.
(c) Means of identification—e.g. blaze or paint mark.

3. Conditions
These will depend on local conditions but may include the following points:
(a) Treatment of 'lop and top' (branches and tree tops).
(b) Repair of damage to fences, gates, roads, drains.
(c) Charge for damage to other trees, or for cutting unmarked trees.
(d) Liability for damage to machinery and personal injury (adequate insurance is essential).
(e) Timing of operations.

4. Price
(a) Lump sum, or paid on out-turn.
(b) Terms of payment.

5. Signatures
(a) Owner, contractor.

Small-sized Produce and Non-timber Products

Commercial timber operations rarely consider material of less than 7 cm (3 inches) diameter which is generally left in the forest or at the roadside as 'forest residue'. Farmers, however, are often in a good position to exploit a variety of local markets for such produce, such as pea/bean sticks, tree and hedging stakes, rails, birch for horse jumps and hazel coppice for walking-sticks. The list is endless and the ingenious can

Harvesting operations

(*left*) Plate 8.5 Felling a mature beech tree.

(*below*)
Plate 8.6 Shortwood extraction of hardwood pulp.

(*above*) Plate 8.7
Tree-length extraction of
pine thinnings.

Plate 8.8   Snedding oak
thinnings.

Plate 8.9   Split chestnut fencing stakes beside a coppice stool.

Plate 8.10   A 'higgler' splitting ash rails.

Plate 8.11 Pointing round fence stakes: the portable saw is driven by the tractor pto.

Plate 8.12 Peeling spruce poles: the bark is collected and sold for equestrian areas.

often obtain higher values for these items than for bulk markets. Small-sized material can also be chipped (along with larger produce) for use as fuel in purpose-built stoves. Some of these uses are illustrated in Plates 8.9–8.12.

Non-timber products include bark (for bedding, footpaths, mulching), Christmas trees, and foliage for floral displays and wreaths. Sporting rents should also be mentioned as a potential source of woodland income and some farmers may be in a position to charge the public for woodland walks at times of the year when flowers are particularly attractive. There may also be the possibility of caravan parks or camping sites.

TIMBER MEASUREMENT

There are two reasons why it is necessary to measure timber:

- valuation—to assess the capital value of a woodland asset;
- management—to plan the ongoing production from thinning and felling.

Every farm should have a woodland Working Plan which identifies individual stands and describes them in standard terms (as outlined in Chapter 10). Yield Class should be included so that the standing volume can be estimated from Yield Tables; valuation is then a matter of deciding on an appropriate mean standing value per cubic metre. This will take account of all the factors affecting unit values that have already been discussed, which vary from farm to farm: an approximate guide to the value of standing timber can be derived from Table 8.3. Valuation of individual standing trees is a skilled business because of the uncertainties involved in estimating both quantity and quality, which is why potentially valuable timber is generally bought 'at stump' or 'at roadside'.

Yield Class can be assessed quite simply for existing crops by using graphs of *age* and *top height* which are published in Forestry Commission Field Book 2. Some examples are shown in Figure 8.4. Age may be known from records, obtained by counting annual rings on a cut stump, or approximated from stem diameter (Table 8.4).

Top height
'Top height' is a forestry term defined as the average total height of the largest-diameter trees in a stand—excluding edge trees which are often abnormal in shape. The simplest method of measuring height is to use a

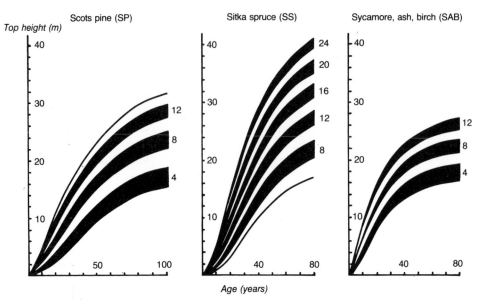

Crown copyright (Field Book 2), reproduced by permission of the Forestry Commission.

Note: (i) Consult FC Field Book 2 for other species.
     (ii) Sycamore, ash and birch are combined because they have similar growth patterns.

Figure 8.4   Examples of age/height curves for estimating Yield Class.

Table 8.4. Estimation of age from tree diameter

Species	Average diameter at breast height (cm)					
	10	20	30	40	50	60+
Beech	35	55	75	95	115	140+
Oak	30	50	70	90	120	150+
Ash, sycamore } Cherry, walnut }	20	30	40	60		
Common alder, birch	15	25	35		*years taken*	
Pine	20	40	60	80	*to reach a*	
Spruce	25	40	55	80	*particular*	
Larch	15	30	45	70	*diameter*	

Note: Diameter growth depends on:
    (i) Stocking—open-grown trees, once established, will grow up to 50 per cent faster in diameter than those in closed woodland.
    (ii) Site quality—ages shown are average values, i.e. what might be expected on reasonably drained Grade 4 land; faster and slower growth will occur on better and poorer sites.
    (iii) Species—on the best sites grey, Italian and red alders can grow up to twice as fast as common (black) alder.

Adapted with kind permission of ADAS and the Forestry Commission from *Practical Work in Farm Woods*.

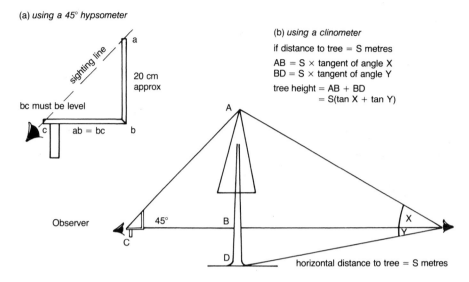

(a) *using a 45° hypsometer*

sighting line

a

20 cm approx

bc must be level

c   ab = bc   b

Observer   45°   C

(b) *using a clinometer*

if distance to tree = S metres

AB = S × tangent of angle X
BD = S × tangent of angle Y

tree height = AB + BD
            = S(tan X + tan Y)

A

B

D

X

Y

horizontal distance to tree = S metres

Since AB = BC
Tree height = (distance to tree) + (height of eye above ground level)

Operation (a) walk backwards or forwards until top of tree coincides with sighting line; the observer should be
standing on the same level as the tree base

Figure 8.5   Measurement of tree height.

home-made 45° hypsometer; an example is shown in Figure 8.5a. Alternatively a clinometer can be used in which case the tangents of the angles to top and bottom of the tree need to be found (Figure 8.5b). The distance from the observer to the tree may be measured with a tape or estimated by pacing. If you want to invest in a purpose-built instrument calibrated in tree height (cost about £70) consult a specialist forestry supplier.

Five to ten of the fattest trees should be measured in each stand and the average height used to estimate Yield Class. If you are planning for an area of bare land or if the existing trees are younger than first thinning stage (Table 8.1) measure trees in an adjacent woodland or ask a local forester for his opinion of the potential Yield Class.

Some woodland may contain a small number of mature trees in woody scrub, or there may be individuals or groups of trees which cannot be assessed by applying Yield Class. A rough estimate of volume can be obtained from tree diameter (Table 8.5). Tree diameter is measured at 1.3 m above ground level ('breast height'—thus DBH) with a girth tape calibrated in diameter, available from specialist forestry suppliers and many chainsaw retailers. A more accurate estimate of volume can be obtained once the tree is felled by placing the tape around the mid-point of the section concerned (see Figure 8.6) and using the following formula:

$$\text{Volume } (m^3) = \frac{\text{cross-sectional area}}{\text{at mid-point}} (m^2) \times \text{length } (m)$$

$$V = \left(\frac{\pi D^2}{4} \times \frac{1}{10,000}\right) L$$

where D (cm) = diameter at midpoint
and L (m) = length.

Volumes based on mid diameter and length are tabulated in Forestry Commission Booklet 26.

Table 8.5. Estimation of tree volume from diameter

Tree diameter at breast height (cm)	Estimated tree volume (m³, overbark)	
	Conifers	Broadleaves
5	0.01	0.01
10	0.04	0.04
15	0.1	0.1
20	0.25	0.25
25	0.45	0.4
30	0.7	0.6
35	1.0	0.9
40	1.5	1.2
45	2.0	1.5
50	2.5	1.9
60	3.6	2.6
70	4.6	3.3
80		4.2
100		6.0

Note: (i) Figures are approximate: differences in tree shape may cause variations of up to 50%.
  (ii) Volume of branchwood is not included. See Table 3.2.
  (iii) 1 cm diameter = 0.31 in Quarter Girth
    1 m³ = 27.7 Hoppus feet (35 true cubic feet).

Adapted with kind permission of ADAS and the Forestry Commission from *Practical Work in Farm Woods*.

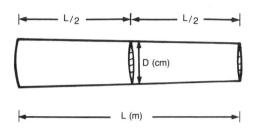

Figure 8.6   Estimating the volume of a felled tree.

Hoppus measure

In the hardwood trade (and for some large softwood logs) buyers and contractors still use the old Hoppus measure. Log volume in Hoppus feet (generally abbreviated simply to 'Hoppus') is derived as follows:

$$\text{Hoppus Volume} = \frac{(\text{mid Quarter Girth})^2}{144} \times \text{Length}$$

where quarter girth and length are measured in inches and feet respectively. A different girth tape is used, calibrated in quarter girth (QG) rather than diameter, and the cross-sectional area is approximated by squaring the QG and dividing by 144.

1 Hoppus foot =   1.27 true cubic feet
and 1 cubic metre = 27.74 'Hoppus feet'.

It is obviously essential to be clear which unit is being used when discussing prices, since timber merchants tend to refer simply to prices 'per cube'. Moderate-quality sycamore butts fetching 'one pound a cube' at roadside might sound poor value until you realise that means approximately £28 per cubic metre, or perhaps £25 per tonne.

The volume of branchwood in mature broadleaves may be considerable, 20–30 per cent of stem volume for woodland trees and up to 100 per cent for open-grown trees (see Table 3.2). Such material is normally cut to a standard length and stacked at roadside. The traditional stack measure is the 'cord' where four-foot lengths are built into a stack of height four feet and length eight feet (128 cubic feet stacked volume, approximately 80 cubic feet solid volume).

References for Further Reading and Suppliers

See Appendix 2.

Chapter 9

WOODLANDS AND FARMING STRATEGY

THE FINAL chapters deal with the planning of farm woodland, firstly on a long-term strategic level and secondly on a short-term operational level. This chapter discusses the potential timber production from different grades of land and the decisions regarding which areas and what type of tree planting are the most appropriate for a given farm enterprise.

The success of the Common Agricultural Policy in creating such large surpluses of agricultural produce in the European Community has placed farmers in a dilemma. Should they respond by reducing inputs, taking land out of production or diversifying into new products? Which is the best response to maintain farm incomes? The National Farmers' Union policy document 'Farming Trees' considers that farm woodland is a viable alternative land use in all areas of Britain, provided that annual payments are available during the initial period of twenty to thirty years when cash flow from a tree crop is negative. This concept, first suggested in Article 20 of the EC's Agricultural Structures Regulation (1985) which was not adopted by the UK, has recently been endorsed by a clear statement of intent from the government (Mr M. Jopling, March 1987) as part of a package of proposals aiming to diversify the rural economy.

The basic question for a farmer thinking about tree planting and tree cropping to diversify an agricultural enterprise is how to maintain a steady income when tree crops have such a variable cash-flow pattern. This problem is greatest on marginal upland farms where the constraint of poorer land quality limits the range of possible land-use options compared with lowland farms, as illustrated in Figure 9.1.

Land Capability for Agriculture and Forestry

Land capability for agriculture is classified differently in Scotland from the rest of Britain but there is broad equivalence between the classes

140

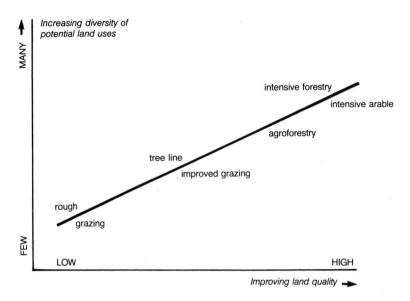

Figure 9.1   Relation between land quality and potential land use.

and grades for lowland areas. Table 9.1 attempts to interpret these classifications in terms of potential timber production, using Yield Class as the measure of tree yield (see page 119). The ranges of Yield Class given are based on experience and intended only as a guide; they assume an appropriate choice of species but are still subject to variation in local site conditions and management input. The low end of the range should be used for exposed or higher-elevation sites in a given land grade or class.

Table 9.1. Potential forestry production in relation to land quality for agriculture

| Land quality for agriculture | | Yield Class | |
E & W[1]	S[2]	Broadleaves	Conifers
Grade 1	Class 1	8–12	20+
2	2	6–10	12–18
3	3	4– 8	10–16
4	4	2– 6	8–14
5	5–7	less than 4	6–12

[1] England and Wales: Resource Planning Group, Land and Water Service, MAFF.
[2] Scotland: Macaulay Land Use Research Institute, Aberdeen.

Land Use Planning

The optimum allocation of land to agriculture and forestry uses depends on the following factors:

1. Land quality.
2. Finance and taxation.
3. Broad environmental objectives.
4. Personal opinion.
5. Existing land use and enterprise mix.

Land quality

Although there are examples of land improvement where operations such as drainage can permanently raise its productive potential, most land use planning is constrained by unalterable climatic, topographic and soil factors. This not only dictates which agricultural crops or tree species are suitable but also the level of integration between farming and woodland. On the best land, for example, 100 per cent arable usage may be possible (though not necessarily desirable from an environmental viewpoint). As land quality becomes poorer there is likely to be an increasing percentage of land unsuitable for agriculture, such as steep, wet or stony areas. Grade (or class) 4 land is capable of producing only a narrow range of crops, being suitable primarily for grassland enterprises with short cropping breaks, and all poorer land is suited only to improved grassland or rough grazing. On these types of land (grade 4 or worse) woodland can play an important rôle in providing shelter, and in some areas can provide a higher financial return than agriculture, once the crop becomes productive. (Problems of financing the initial establishment phase are discussed in the next section.) In a study of thirteen farms in the hills and uplands, it was found that on average 15 per cent of the extensive grazing could be planted without reducing the size of the sheep enterprise (see reference in Appendix 2).

The previous paragraph gives the conventional view of trees being only suitable for the poorest land. However, exceptions to this general rule may develop in four areas—agroforestry, wood energy, high-quality hardwood timber crops, and trees associated with non-agricultural enterprises.

Agroforestry is a general term to describe systems in which farming and forestry are consciously combined and actively managed at the same time and on the same piece of land. In some literature it is used synonymously with 'farm forestry' but it is preferable to restrict the latter to systems in which the farming and the tree crop, though integrated within one proprietorship, are not practised on the same piece of land.

There is nothing new about the idea of combining forestry with other land uses, especially the grazing of animals under trees and even the interplanting of trees with arable crops. Such systems have very long histories indeed. Recently, however, there has been a resurgence of interest in various multiple-cropping systems. In many tropical countries the new concern is in response to increasing need for both food and firewood; in many hungry countries fuel is as scarce as food itself and the destruction of the forest for firewood (combined with clearance for food crops, and overgrazing) is the basic environmental decline which triggers famine and disaster. In Britain, and indeed over most of Europe, the interest in agroforestry lies in the opportunity it may provide for farmers to diversify their production from the land and perhaps to switch some of their production from food to wood over a period. This requires conditions suitable for growing timber of reasonable quality, as illustrated in Plates 9.1 and 9.2, for which grade 3 or 4 land might be suitable.

The recent interest in wood energy crops in Britain was stimulated by the energy crisis of the early 1970s. In countries like Sweden and Ireland, with relatively low population densities and limited resources of fossil fuels, the production of energy from short coppice rotations of willow or other species may be practicable. Sweden, for example, is planning to replace 20 per cent of its oil imports by planting short-rotation crops. Although the European Parliament wishes to divert some farmland to energy crops it seems unlikely that major developments of this nature will occur in the United Kingdom until energy costs from other sources rise considerably. Good soils and flat land are required to achieve high production and enable mechanised working, and this brings energy crops into potential conflict with arable agriculture. Some peat areas may also be suitable, despite problems of drainage and nutrition, particularly at low altitudes as in parts of Ireland and western Britain.

High-quality hardwood timber crops are less demanding than energy crops in terms of land quality but still represent a predominantly lowland enterprise. Ash and walnut in particular grow best on fertile loams and 'cricket bat' willow is grown along banks near to constantly flowing water. English oak prefers heavy loams and clays, while beech can tolerate more freely drained base-rich soils. All these species could be grown on potential arable land. Conifer crops would yield more in financial terms than broadleaves on many lowland sites but would meet strong opposition on environmental grounds. However, small areas of conifers cropped for foliage—possibly worked on an agri-silvicultural system (Plate 9.3)—might be acceptable. Trees associated with non-agricultural enterprises include amenity planting for recreational facilities,

Plate 9.1 An example of agri-silviculture: intercropping of undersown wheat and conifers.

Plate 9.2 Silvi-pastoralism: sheep under widely spaced poplars in Wales.

Plate 9.3   An example of agri-silviculture: silver fir grown for its foliage and inter-cropped with an arable crop on a German farm.

for example. This is likely to involve a wide range of species with management placing timber production lowest in its list of objectives.

Finance and taxation

These subjects have been discussed thoroughly in Chapter 7. This book seeks to encourage farmers to carry out woodland work themselves rather than selling or leasing land to another person or agency interested in a forestry enterprise. Although the latter option can provide capital to invest in improving a farm it represents a major decision of land use planning which inevitably restricts future planning of land allocation.

Broad environmental objectives

These aspects were mentioned in Chapter 6. People are becoming increasingly interested in environmental issues, despite being largely urban based, and consequently land use planning on the farm must consider its effect on the landscape, wildlife habitat and recreational pursuits. In common with taxation these represent institutional constraints on the land manager and it is likely that they will increase (particularly if odd cases of 'insensitive' land use changes continue) perhaps in the form of planning guidelines and planting licences, even if agriculture and forestry remain outside the formal planning legislation. The Farming (Forestry) and Wildlife Groups (FWAGs), many of which now employ a local adviser, exist to strengthen the links that exist between the farming community and the conservation and amenity 'lobbies'. Your local FWAG officer should be able to advise you on the necessary consultation that must be undertaken prior to planting, for example.

Personal opinion
No comment is really appropriate here except to say that this can turn out to be the most important influence on your decision. This point is highlighted in the next section.

Existing land use and enterprise mix
One important feature of land use planning is to assess the various factors affecting allocation to different enterprises and prepare a theoretical plan *before* considering the existing situation. This will generally lead to a better compromise being achieved than if the latter is allowed too much influence in deciding on an optimal solution. Clearly this is easier to achieve in theory than in practice and it may be that you have no wish to alter the basic pattern of farming that you follow. It is however an interesting intellectual exercise, and it may illustrate to you just how much your management decisions are influenced by your personal preference.

DECIDING ON THE BEST LAND ALLOCATION

A discussion of suitable criteria and methods for optimum land allocation could occupy a complete chapter, or indeed another book. What is presented here are two examples of an economic approach which allows land use decisions to be made on an objective basis. (Some readers may wish to leave this theoretical section and continue with Chapter 10.)

The first considers the economic outcome of allocating different proportions of an area of hill land to either sheep grazing or commercial forestry. The area is divided into a grid of square blocks (each 10 hectares) which are each classified in terms of potential productivity, using vegetation and soil type to estimate stock-carrying capacity and Yield Class. The position of existing access and fencing is noted and a list made of current operational costings. Each block is then allocated to either forestry or sheep grazing within certain constraints such as the need for all agricultural land to be contiguous and large enough to constitute a viable farm unit. A range of different allocations is then assessed on financial criteria, including the appropriate roading and fencing requirements. It is then possible to determine objectively whether, for example, one should aim for high stocking rates on a relatively small area of good land and have a large area of poor land in forestry; or lower stocking rates on a larger area of poor land, with a small area of good land in forestry (see Figure 9.2). The effects of land improvement and changes in market values can also be investigated.

Use of this model has shown that in some circumstances the integration of sheep grazing and tree growing (farm forestry, not agroforestry) can give a higher return than using it only for one or the other industry. It should be noted that the proprietor still has to choose between different land allocations which appear to offer similar financial returns and that non-productive considerations such as amenity and conservation may well influence his decision.

The second is an agroforestry example. The economics of agroforestry are founded in joint product theory. A manager may have a piece of land that is suitable for growing both grass and timber, and techniques and resources are available for growing both. His problem is to decide whether to grow grass for animal feeding or timber, or some combination of the two. By applying a given amount of labour, fertiliser, etc., to the fixed area of land, the manager may produce on each hectare either, say, 3.5 tonnes of dry grass from an open field or 11 cubic metres of timber from closed woodland (see Figure 9.3), or combinations of grass and timber shown as a 'production contour' line linking these points on the axes of the graph. If the amounts of variable inputs (labour etc.) are increased on each hectare, new 'contours' of alternative product combinations are developed to the right of the first, up to the highest of 12 tonnes of dry grass or 19 cubic metres of timber. Each curve represents the range of product combinations, from only grass to only timber, offered at a single cost level. The manager's problem is to select the best combination.

The selection of the combination of products to give the highest gross margin return needs a measurement of the incomes as well as the costs of production. Both dry grass and timber are goods traded in the market so their prices can be used. The quantities of each that exchange in the market for the same amount of money may be connected on the graph to show a 'market line'. Each line shows all the combinations of grass and timber that can be traded for the same amount of cash. Since

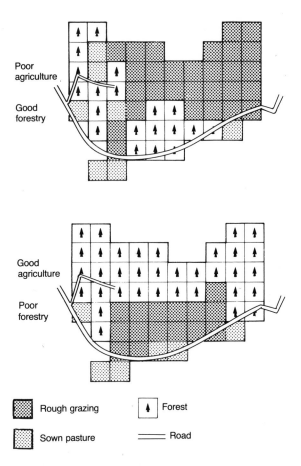

Poor
agriculture

Good
forestry

Good
agriculture

Poor
forestry

Rough grazing   ▲ Forest

Sown pasture   ═══ Road

Reproduced from the HFRO Biennial Report (1979–81) with permission from the Macaulay Land Use Research Institute (formerly Hill Farming Research Organisation).

Figure 9.2   Alternative land allocations to sheep grazing and forestry (the land quality decreases away from the road).

2 tonnes cost double 1 tonne, and 4 tonnes cost twice as much as two, these market lines are straight and parallel (Figure 9.4). In a more complex situation one or both of the products may not be traded in the market, to provide shelter or wildlife habitat for example; in these instances the 'market lines' would be curved and difficult to draw.

The manager, at each level of inputs, wants to achieve the combination that would give the highest gross margin or greatest benefit.

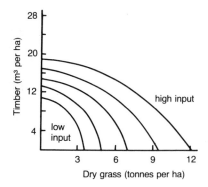

Figure 9.3   Production contours showing yields per hectare of dry grass and timber. (Five levels of input, each line comprising all possible combinations of the two products at that level of input.)

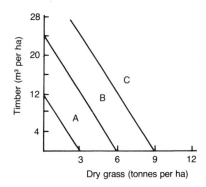

Figure 9.4   Market lines showing combinations of dry grass and timber for three levels of income— A, B, and C. (Each straight line shows products that trade in the market for the same amount: 6 tonnes of hay has equal value to 24 m³ of timber.)

That will be at the point where the 'production contour' just touches the furthest right market line; where the slopes of the two are the same the marginal cost and the marginal revenue are equal. By connecting all the points at which a curve just touches its market line, the manager finds the best set of combinations of grass and timber at the various input levels he must consider seriously (see Figure 9.5). Finally, for each of that set, the total cost and total revenue must be calculated; the point at which there is maximum separation of these values represents the best solution to the manager's problem, that is to say, the greatest gross margin or greatest benefit (Figure 9.6).

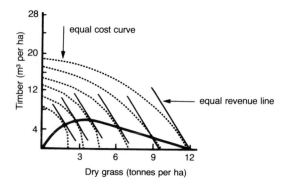

Figure 9.5   Best combinations of products for highest gross margins at different input levels. (The thick solid line joins the points where an equal cost curve and equal revenue line touch, each of which is the best combination at its own input level. The overall best combination must lie on the thick solid line, or 'expansion path', but it is not yet clear which point is most profitable.)

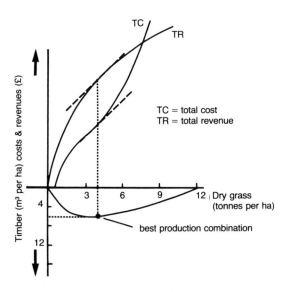

Figure 9.6   Joint production for maximum net revenue. (The upper half of the graph shows the total cost and total revenue of each combination of production. The production at which there is widest separation between the two lines suggests the best combination (i.e. best gross profit). Vertical projection downwards (dotted line) to the lower graph—a mirror image of the thick solid line in Figure 9.5—allows the best combination to be read off).

This suggested analysis has been greatly simplified by ignoring the fact that trees take much longer to grow than one crop of hay, and by supposing that the manager would know both the combinations of products available at each input cost and the relative market prices in years ahead, in order to make the comparisons. In practice the result is sensitive to differences in the response of land to environmental influences and to changes in the market prices of the goods. The 'production contours' for two distinct areas may have quite different shapes (Figures 9.7 and 9.8). If the same scales and prices are used, the graph of the first would tell the manager to grow grass and that of the

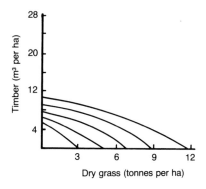

Figure 9.7   Production contours for land best in grass. (On this land there is a far better response to increased inputs in grass production than in timber. It is best to keep such land under grass. Only if timber became extraordinarily valuable would a straight revenue line touch the graphs at points other than on the grass axis.)

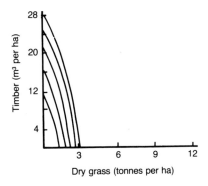

Figure 9.8   Production contours for land best in forestry. (On this land the system responds to increased inputs far more strongly in timber output than in grass. It would be better to keep this land in timber than to attempt a mixed management. Only if grass became extraordinarily valuable would anyone try to grow grass here.)

second to grow timber. In other words for most goods this type of analysis appears ultimately to favour one product or another when the investment of input factors is increased. Experience at both the individual farm and regional development levels has shown managers progressively abandoning secondary products and concentrating on a chosen principal one which offers the best returns. The selection of the combination of products and the investment level which offers the widest separation of the total cost and total revenue curves is not simple; nor is the best option likely to be permanent. The result is very sensitive to changes in price, changes in non-market values and changes in production curves.

The implications of this discussion for current farming problems may be important. Agroforestry systems may prove to be impermanent, though useful and appropriate in the medium term, because on a given type of land one element of the joint system offers a larger response than the other (or others) to each unit of investment, producing skewed 'production contours' rather than symmetrical ones. On fertile soils at low elevation an extra unit of investment will yield more in farming than in trees which is why grade 1 land is used for farming rather than forestry.

The attraction and importance of agroforestry at the present lies in the possibility that it offers the farmer the advantage of diversifying his production into wood while avoiding the loss of income that would normally follow a simple transfer of land from traditional grazing to traditional forestry. Agroforestry may prove to be a means for the farmer to achieve some farm-forestry (as already defined) without the pain of a sharp reduction of income; as such it would be a transitional system rather than a permanent one. When the trees of the first agroforestry crop are mature, it seems likely that the farmer, if he finds timber commanding good prices, will move towards a completely forestry system on part of his land rather than re-create the mixed agroforestry system.

References for Further Reading

See Appendix 2.

Chapter 10

WOODLAND WORK AND THE FARM BUSINESS

IT IS ALWAYS annoying to see one (or more!) of the service industries digging up a newly re-surfaced road. 'You'd have thought they could have co-ordinated their planning more efficiently,' is the inevitable comment, although everyone is guilty of bad planning at some time or other. By analogy, this illustrates a major principle underlying woodland work and the farm business—they must be planned together and not in isolation, in order to achieve maximum success and minimum conflict. The timing of some woodland operations—such as planting and weeding—is critical whereas the timing of others—such as harvesting—may be flexible over several years. Insufficient thought over even a small planting programme can double establishment costs by requiring the replacement of losses due to poor plant handling or lack of protection. Similarly it is best not to harvest mature timber next to a newly erected fence!

Time and Labour Input

Before getting down to planning, it is necessary to assess the time and labour input of woodland operations, and how these fit into the life of a tree crop and into any twelve-month period. Table 10.1 outlines the operations throughout the rotation of two contrasting crops, illustrating the concentration of work in the establishment period. Table 10.2 provides a simple calendar of woodland work in British conditions, highlighting those operations where timing is critical for success. Table 10.3 gives some typical output figures per man per day; this is only intended as an initial guide because conditions and operators vary so much: you can build up your own figures from experience. Plates 10.1– 10.10 illustrate some of the operations.

Since the timing of woodland work is generally not critical—the exceptions being planting and weeding—there is considerable scope for

153

Table 10.1. Typical woodland operations through the life of a tree crop

Operation	Upland conifers	Lowland broadleaves
	(the age of crop is shown in brackets)	
Establishment		
Ground preparation	plough (0)	clear brambles, spray grass (0)
Protection	fence (0)	tree shelters (1)
Planting	2 m spacing (1)	3 m spacing (1)
Beating-up	15% of planting (2)	15% of planting (2)
Maintenance		
Weeding	partial (2, 3)	pre-planting (0) around trees (1–5)
Cleaning	—	release from woody competition (10–15)
Brashing	access only (19)	—
Pruning	—	partial, after alternate thinnings (25–65)
Harvesting		
Thinning	every 5 years (20–45)	every 5 to 10 years (25–95)
Felling	clearfell (50)	group fellings (50–150).

Checklist for each woodland visit:
What was planned to be done?
What should be done?
What must be done?

employment of farm labour when other work is slack, particularly in the winter months. The advantage of using farm labour is that it will encourage an understanding of the woodland enterprise and increase the chances of genuine co-ordination and integration with the agricultural enterprise. Opportunities for timely action will be spotted (such as freeing young trees from a dense patch of weed growth) and new ideas for using farm equipment and materials will be formed, adding to both efficiency and enjoyment. For example, fertiliser bags can be used to suppress weed growth around young trees on suitable sites.

If farm labour is not readily available it will be necessary to explore alternative sources. Co-operation with neighbours is one possibility, or part-time employment of local forestry workers, or use of contractors. Woodland operations require skill for safety and efficiency, and the lack of forestry skills among farm labour may be the main reason for using

Table 10.2. A suggested calendar for woodland work

September	Site preparation for spring planting. Clearance, drainage, fencing, etc.
October	Harvesting; coppice-cutting from October. *'Back-end' planting (timing depends on location and season).
November	Harvesting, ground preparation, planting broadleaves.
December	Brashing, pruning, cleaning, application of granular herbicide.
January	Fence and drain maintenance. Snow assists a check on rabbit or deer populations.
February	Ground preparation, *planting broadleaves (lowland sites)
March	Ground preparation, *planting
April	*Planting, beating-up, harvesting; coppice cutting up to April.
May	*Weeding (as and when required to relieve competition).
June	—
July	Harvesting—easier access after farm crops, control of woody weeds.
August	Road construction or improvement.

* Operations where timing is critical, depending on weather conditions and location.

contractors. It is always advisable to be selective in the choice of contractor, observing or enquiring about workmanship and safety equipment beforehand and sharing knowledge of good contractors. There are opportunities for co-operation between farmer and contractor once a good relationship has been built up. Payment in kind is one example, where timber or cordwood might be taken in exchange for thinning or felling. (Such arrangements work best where only low-value produce is involved.) Cash-flow problems may confront both farmer and contractor and can be offset by the contractor agreeing not to be paid until some material is sold, or conversely, the owner paying an initial sum on account once the work has started. Payment for firewood felling in the summer might provide a contractor with work during a slack

Table 10.3. Labour guide for woodland operations

Operation	Typical output per man per day
Clearing	0.05 ha (by hand); 0.25 ha (mechanical, chemical).
Draining	50–100 m (mechanical digger).
Fencing	30–50 m.
Ploughing	0.5–1.0 ha.
Planting	250 (pit); 500 (notch); 1000 (after ploughing).
Tree shelters	150 (erection after planting).
Weeding	up to 0.05 ha (hand); 1–2 ha (mechanical, chemical).
Cleaning	0.25 ha (hand); 0.5 ha (brushcutter).
Brashing	100–250 trees (less for spruce, more for pine/larch).
Pruning	25–50 trees (depending on height pruned).
Coppice cutting	0.02 ha (small sizes); 0.05 ha (larger sizes).
Tree felling	3.5 tonnes (m³)—includes debranching.
Extraction	15 tonnes (m³)—depends on distance to road.

N.B. Work in pairs for safety

Equipment, methods and protective clothing are described in a series of free leaflets obtainable from The Forestry Safety Council, 231 Corstorphine Road, Edinburgh EH12 7AT.

Plate 10.1   Maintenance of deer fencing round a young plantation.

period and cause less damage to tracks and rides, even though the farmer would need to wait until winter for the best sale price.

Training and equipment

Training in woodland operations is organised by the Forestry Training Council and the Agricultural Training Board (addresses can be found in Appendix 3). Similar courses are run by some Local Authority Agricultural Colleges and a list of registered courses is published by MAFF. Codes of practice for the use of herbicides—which must now conform to regulations in the Food and Environment Protection Act—are available from the Forestry Safety Council, and contractors applying herbicides should have a certificate of competence.

Chainsaw work, extraction and application of herbicide should only be undertaken by trained operators, including farm staff who have completed an appropriate course, with full protective clothing (as described in free guides published by the Forestry Safety Council). Planting, mechanical weeding and marking trees for thinning are skilled rather than dangerous operations and would benefit from experienced supervision. For cleaning, brashing, pruning and coppicing small-size material using hand tools, training is not essential, although eye protection is advisable. A specially designed curved pruning saw makes that operation and brashing much easier but otherwise standard hand tools can be used.

The most widely used piece of equipment is the chainsaw and modern chainsaws are lighter, quieter and safer than older models. If woodland work is planned, purchase a suitable model rather than relying on the typically large, old farm saw kept for every eventuality.

Machinery Input

Agricultural tractors and trailers can be used for transporting materials, plants and small-sized produce. Most farm tractors, however, are not designed or equipped with winches to extract larger timber and a forest tractor specialist should be consulted about modifications to existing machinery for forest use. It must also be emphasised that extraction of large timber is skilled and potentially dangerous work for which training is essential.

If it is decided to use farm machinery for harvesting, versatility is obviously a key principle. There is generally no need to consider expensive purpose-built commercial forestry harvesting machinery but rather aim at a tractor–trailer combination which can carry out a number of jobs. A drawbar trailer can be easily left in a wood for loading while the tractor does another job; equally it can be unhitched if it gets bogged down while the tractor goes for help! A hydraulic crane mounted on the trailer can be used for loading and unloading a variety of commodities, including timber, without the extra strengthening and resultant 'clumsiness' of a tractor-mounted crane. Timber winches can

Plate 10.2 Planting two-year-old oak transplants (1+1) using a garden spade.

Plate 10.3 Brashing Scots pine in preparation for a line thinning.

be mounted for the winter months and removed during the summer and PTO-driven saws and chippers can be used for cutting and pointing stakes and processing fuelwood.

Farm woodlands are typically small and scattered, and small amounts of work in different places mean a large amount of unproductive movement time. Work co-ordination and machinery sharing between neighbouring farms can help to reduce costs. There will also be some larger blocks of woodland where it will pay to employ contractors with specialised machinery. Once again, co-operation between neighbouring farms to provide the contractor with three weeks' work in one location rather than three days should reduce costs—though you may need to argue the point! Alternatively several farms could share hire charges or spread the cost of purchasing specialised equipment.

Management Input

At the outset there are two important points to be made about the planning of woodland operations: firstly, the necessary management skills already exist on the farm, i.e. getting the best out of limited resources. Secondly, because of the totally different time scale, it is best to have a separate Woodland Plan which can be amended every five years or so to take account of changing circumstances. An example of a Woodland Plan is included at the end of the chapter. Because trees have a long life span, it is wise to start with long-term questions and work back to specific short-term action.

1. Purpose of woodland
The first thing to do (as mentioned in Chapter 2) is to consider existing woodland and decide what purpose you wish it to serve—wood products, shelter, conservation, etc.—and list these in order of priority. The Woodland Checklist in the packet of leaflets called 'Practical Work in Farm Woods' prepared jointly by ADAS and the Forestry Commission will be useful. If new woodland is planned the same exercise will be necessary for these areas also. It is impossible to plan anything without knowing what you want to achieve.

2. Description of woodland
The most useful single document is an accurate map, called a Stock Map, showing the woodland blocks, existing and planned. The equivalent of a farmer's field or paddock is the forester's *compartment* (cpt.) and each woodland block should be allocated a compartment number. If the trees within a block differ in age or species or condition, you can divide the compartment into *sub-compartments* (sub-cpt.) which are

Plate 10.4   The effect of chemical weeding (Propyzamide): oak seedling, one year after planting.

allocated a lower-case letter, e.g. sub-cpts. 3a, 3b and 3c. (Each sub-compartment will contain a *stand* of trees—the forester's term for an area which is more-or-less uniform in respect of age and species composition, tree condition and growth rate.) The world is divided into 'lumpers' and 'splitters' but simplicity is normally best so only subdivide if it is really necessary.

The scale of a Stock Map should be at least 1:10,000 (roughly six inches to the mile) and you can obtain the relevant Ordnance Survey (OS) sheets from a bookseller. Larger scales are appropriate for small woods to put in more detail—these can be sketched, using pacing for measuring distance, on the basis of the OS map. Stock Maps provide the following information directly:

—location
—boundaries, configuration
—area (record to nearest 0.1 ha)
—topography and elevation (from contours)
—access (note all-weather and dry-weather tracks)
—some important features, e.g. public footpaths, pylon lines, other way-leaves, ancient monuments, etc.

Plate 10.5 Pruning selected oak trees up to about 5 metres to increase the value of the butt log.

Plate 10.6 Marking a thinning in a sixty-year-old oak stand; note the poor form of the trees marked for cutting.

Plate 10.7 Thinning a thirty-year-old oak stand.

Plate 10.8 Cutting Christmas trees.

Plate 10.9 Roe deer control from a high seat.

Plate 10.10 Squirrel trapping: the damage on the beech tree is probably caused by careless extraction, but similar damage is caused by squirrels on smaller stems.

Stock Maps can also be annotated to show the following information:

—soil type (heavy/light, wet/dry, deep/shallow/stony)
—exposure to wind, ground vegetation
—type of tree crop (species, planting year, Yield Class)
—other features (e.g. buildings, bridges, drains, fencing).

Planting year is more useful than age (because age keeps changing) and abbreviations can be used for species to keep the map simple (see Appendix 1). For example 'NS p75' means Norway spruce planted in 1975, and '4/2.4' means Compartment 4, area 2.4 hectares.

Aerial photographs can be of great assistance in preparing a Stock Map, though beware of taking linear or area measurements from them because they are often not true to scale. They give a useful pictorial image of both farmland and woodland. Purchase black-and-white nine-inch prints at a scale between 1:15,000 and 1:5,000. Enquiries can be made at St. Andrew's House, Edinburgh, or at the Ordnance Survey, Southampton, to see if photocover exists for any particular area (quote the kilometre square required from a 1:50,000 OS map).

In addition to the Stock Map, every sub-compartment or group of sub-compartments should have a record sheet. A simple example is the Woodland Assessment Form in the ADAS/FC leaflets where three sub-compartments, or stands, are placed on one sheet. There is no perfect design for all situations but the intention is to provide a concise statement of the tree crop and what action is intended during the period of the Woodland Plan. (The acid test for a good form is how easily the information can be understood by another person!) Compartment records are necessary because of the long time scale of woodland operations. They can also serve to record actual as well as planned operations, and costs or revenues, and thus help to assess progress and provide information for a revised or new plan.

Essential information on a Compartment Record

• Identification—name of wood, number (+ letter) of (sub) cpt.
• Area—to nearest 0.1 ha.
• Tree species—proportion (by area) for mixtures.
• Planting year—estimate from diameter if no records exist.
• Work intended during period of the Woodland Plan.

Additional useful information on a Compartment Record

• Top height. ⎫
• Yield Class. ⎬   *see Chapter 8*
• Stocking. ⎭

- Health, timber quality, wind, fire or animal damage.
- Standing value.
- Work carried out, and when.
- Sporting or other non-timber value.
- Forestry Commission (or other) grant application.

3. Summary of prescriptions

Having identified objectives—in order of priority—and set down how these will be achieved in each woodland area, it is useful to go through the compartment records and extract a *summary table* of work proposed, on an annual basis. This highlights the work to be done each year and ensures that no areas are overlooked. Detailed plans for each year's work can be based on the summary.

The Woodland Plan is best produced as a loose-leaf folder which can be added to, or altered, relatively easily. Because circumstances change—young crops grow into the harvesting stage, old crops need

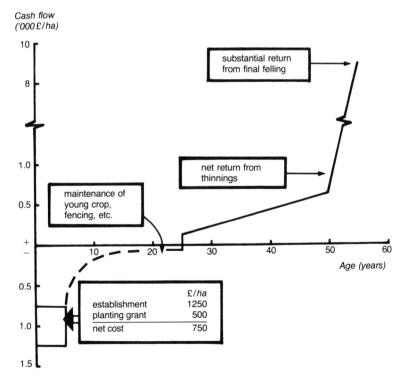

Figure 10.1   Cash flow pattern for even-aged tree crop.

felling and regeneration, markets improve or decline, financial opportunities come and go—it is necessary to revise the plan at regular intervals. Five years is a good period to choose because it fits in with the Forestry Commission grant scheme applications which include a five-year 'Plan of Operations'. The information needed to complete a grant application will be readily available from the Woodland Plan.

Financial Input

Figure 10.1 shows that the cash flow of an even-aged tree crop over one rotation is very irregular, starting with heavy expenditure on establishment and ending with about half the total revenue in one year when the trees are felled. This irregularity also applies to labour, machinery and produce, quite different from most of the farm enterprise. But if

Table 10.4. Contractor's costs for woodland operations

Operation	Unit	Unit cost £(1990)
Establishment		
Ploughing, ripping	hectare	50–75
Drainage (by excavator)	metre	0.4–0.5
Fencing, high tensile, stock	metre	1.6–1.8
+ rabbit netting	metre	+ 0.9–1.1
Planting (2500 trees = 2 m spacing)		
conifers	hectare	175–200
broadleaves	,,	350–400
Labour, notch planting on plough	,,	55–70
screef planting, unploughed	,,	150–200
Planting + erecting tree shelter	tree	1.0–1.3
(including materials)		
Maintenance		
Weeding, chemical	hectare	90–100
hand	,,	100–125
Cleaning (hand)	,,	100–200
Brashing (25%)	,,	75–150
Pruning (in 2 m stages)	tree	0.5–1.0
Harvesting		
Costs depend on tree size, extraction conditions and distance		
Fell and debranch (sned)	m³, tonne	5–15
Extract to roadside	,,	1–5

woodland areas can be organised in such a way that there is a good distribution of ages on the farm, periodic income and expenditure can be more stable. This also happens if the woodland is irregular in structure, or uneven-aged, rather than being made up of even-aged units. If the total area is small it may be impossible to design such a diverse age structure but thought should be given to the effect of age distribution on long-term cash flow.

In the short term, 'financial input' refers to expenditure on (or revenue from) specific operations. Table 10.4 shows a typical contractor's figures, though it should be emphasised that these vary considerably in different circumstances and from year to year. Table 10.3 indicates the labour input required for different operations so that labour costs can be estimated on a man-day basis.

If the woodland structure is designed in such a way that harvesting revenues, establishment costs and planting grants occur in each five-year period the periodic financial return should be positive, albeit modest, for most farm woodlands.

Woodland Plan

We began this book with the statement that its aim was to generate both interest and action. It is therefore wholly appropriate to conclude with an example of a Woodland Plan to re-emphasise the practical necessity of thinking through a woodland enterprise and putting down the essential details in a systematic way. As has been pointed out, trees grow on a much longer time scale than farm crops and this exercise, however simple, is the single most useful action that any woodland manager can carry out. We wish you pleasure and success in your woodland work.

WOODLAND PLAN FOR 'HILL FARM'

(modified from a real plan currently in operation)

1. Purpose of Woodland—Objectives

(a) Maintain good stocking and mixed composition for shelter and amenity around farm buildings.
(b) Operate on a self-financing basis.

2. Description of Woodland and Summary of Work Proposed

(a) Total Area = 1.8 hectares

(b) Stock Map Showing Compartment Layout

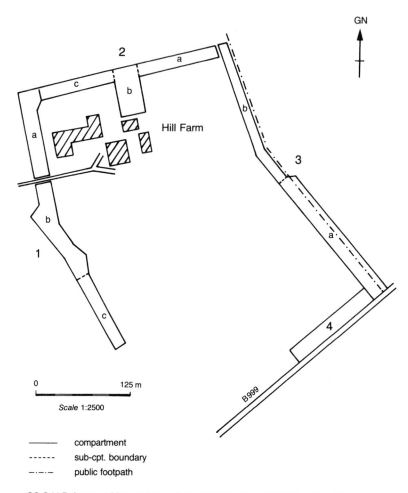

OS Grid Reference of farm buildings is AB 123 456 (OS 1:50 000 Sheet No. X)

(c) Compartment Record

Sub-cpt.	Area(ha)	Species	Planting year	Work proposed (1990–94)
1a	0.2 ⎫	mixed blf	1900 ⎫	fell & restock 0.1 ha
b	0.3 ⎭	and SP	⎭	with broadleaves
c	0.1	SP	1920	thin
2a	0.1	mixed blf		check for elm disease
b	0.2	mainly lime	1885	remove affected trees
c	0.2	mixed blf		
3a	0.3	1:1 mxd. blf/SP	1900	thin if required
b	0.2	2:1 mxd. blf/SP		
4	0.2	SP	1920	fell to raise capital for protection of restocking

Note: Existing crop poorly stocked; moderate-quality SP in Cpt. 4 is the best.
Regenerate Cpts. 1, 2 & 3 over 40 years, approximately 0.2 ha every 5 years, using group felling and replanting with individual tree protection.

3. Budget for 1990–1994

Year	Sub-cpt	Revenue	Expenditure	Cash flow	
1990	4	40 m³ @ £15 (standing sale, SP)		+600	
	1a	10 trees @ £3 (standing sale)	restock 0.1 ha (250 trees + shelters)	+30 −280	+350
1991	1a		beat-up and weed as required	−25	+325
1992	1a		weed as required	−10	+315
1994	1b	15 trees @ £3 (standing sale)	restock 0.1 ha (250 trees + shelters)	+45 −280	+80

Note: (i) Apply for Countryside Commission grant (F.C. grant not applicable because areas too small).
(ii) Felling licence required in 1990 (Cpt. 4); other felling covered by F.C. Plan of Operations.
(iii) Thinning assumed to break even.

References for Further Reading

See Appendix 2.

APPENDIX 1

Notes on the More Important Tree Species
Commonly Found on Farms and Suitable for Farm Planting

Adapted with kind permission of the Forestry Commission from *Forestry
Practice* Forestry Commission bulletin 14 (9th edition).

BROADLEAVES

Species and native country	Conditions justifying selection	Unsuitable conditions	Notes on timber	General remarks and Yield Class* (average YC in brackets)
Oaks: Pedunculate oak (POK), *Quercus robur* L., and Sessile oak (SOK), *Quercus petraea* (Matt.) Lieb. British Isles and Europe	Well-aerated deep fertile loams. Grow well on fertile heavy soils: clays and marls. Strong light demanders. Sessile oak tolerates less rich soils than does Pedunculate oak.	Avoid all shallow, ill-drained or infertile soils, and exposed areas. On lighter sandy soils the timber is prone to shake—longitudinal splits in wood.	Oak is both hard and resistant to abrasion. It has a naturally durable heartwood, but the sapwood needs preservative treatments for exterior uses. Prime clean oak is used for veneers, furniture, gates, flooring and barrel staves for tight cooperage. Lower grades of oak are used for fencing, weather-boarding, engineering, wagon construction and repair, sawn mining timber. Round oak is used for hardwood pulpwood and chipboard. Small poles are valued for cleft or round fence stakes.	Both species are very windfirm. Main species of standard in coppice with standards. Dominant species in over 30% of broadleaved high forest in Britain. Good hedgerow tree. Responds well to growing in tree shelters. 2–8 (4)

* Yield Class (m³/hectare/annum): see Chapter 8 for explanation. Note that no figures are available for species such as elm and lime which are not grown in plantations.

Species	Site requirements	Uses	Notes	Spacing
Beech (Be), *Fagus sylvatica* L. Southern England, South Wales, and Europe	Soils over chalk and limestone. Good loams of all types if well drained. Likes a mild sunny climate. A good shade-bearer. Tolerant of smoke pollution. Useful shelterbelt species, and reasonably tolerant of exposure.	Avoid frost hollows, heavy soils on badly drained sites, leached soils, peats and strongly calcareous soils on which it is inclined to become chlorotic.	Beech has a wider range of indoor uses than any other home-grown hardwood, but is rarely employed out of doors. It is strong, works well to a good finish, and is easily stained. Its uses include furniture, particularly for kitchens and schools, turnery, flooring, veneers, bentwood and pulpwood. It is a good wood for charcoal making and firewood.	Benefits from a nurse on exposed areas; Scots pine is a suitable species. Useful for underplanting. Grey squirrels can be very destructive to young beech. Stem form often poor. Dense planting gives better chance of selecting individuals for final crop. Coppices poorly. 4–10 (6)
Ash (Ash), *Fraxinus excelsior* L. British Isles and Europe	An exacting species which demands good soil conditions rich in nitrogen. Likes sheltered situations and deep calcareous loams, moist but well drained. Thrives on chalk and limestone especially where soil is deep. Benefits from shelter in youth.	Not a suitable species for large-scale planting or for use on open ground. Avoid frost hollows, dry or shallow soils, grassland, heath or moorland, ill-drained ground, heavy clays. Exposed situations are also unsuitable.	Ash has a high resistance to shock and is thus used for oars, hockey sticks and other sports equipment, vehicle framing, tool handles and turnery and furniture. Also for pulpwood and firewood. Well-grown white ash (wood unstained) is a valuable timber.	Plant ash where there is local evidence that first-class timber can be produced. It is uncommon to find suitable conditions except in small patches, and it is necessary to choose these sites with care. Regenerates very freely on any exposed mineral soil; such growth is not a reliable guide to good ash sites. 4–10 (6)

Species and native country	Conditions justifying selection	Unsuitable conditions	Notes on timber	General remarks and Yield Class (average YC in brackets)
Sycamore (Syc), *Acer pseudoplatanus* Central Europe	Fairly frost hardy. Stands exposure and smoke pollution very well. Useful broadleaved species for uplands. Tolerant of a wide range of soils, from fairly acid to calcareous.	As for ash but stands exposure and is more frost hardy.	A white timber especially suitable for use in contact with food (kitchen utensils, butchers' blocks, bread-boards, etc.). A good turnery timber. Figured sycamore is much sought after for veneer and furniture manufacture. Used for pulpwood and firewood.	A useful tree for a windfirm mixture with conifers in shelterbelts. Grey squirrels can be very harmful. Generally vigorous, long-lived tree. Regenerates freely. 4–12 (6)
Sweet chestnut, *Castanea sativa* Mill. Mediterranean	Needs a deep acid soil, and it does best in a sunny, warm climate. Profitable as coppice in the south of England.	Unsuitable on soil of pH > 5.5, frosty or exposed sites, badly drained ground or heavy clays. Timber prone to shake on sandy soils.	Coppice-grown material is used for cleft fencing and hop poles. Sawn timber is similar to oak and wood is naturally durable, used for furniture and coffin boards.	When grown for timber, should not be left to reach very large size owing to risk of shake. 4–10 (6)

Species	Site requirements		Uses	Yield	Remarks
Poplars: (Pop) Black hybrids, *Populus* × *euramericana* (Dode Guinier) P. 'Eugenei' P. 'Gelrica' P. 'Laevigata' P. 'Robusta' P. 'Serotina' Europe	Very exacting; suitable sites are limited. Loamy soils in sheltered situations. Rich alluvial or fen soils, both well drained and well watered. Banks of streams.	Avoid high elevation, exposed sites and shallow soils. Stagnant water is fatal but occasional floods do no harm. Avoid acid peats and heathland.	Large clean poplar was peeled for matches; now only veneer packages (chip baskets). Used for wagon and barrow bottoms because of its high resistance to abrasion. Good pulpwood.	4–16 (8)	Poplar growing is a specialised job. Poplars should be considered for planting when dealing with derelict or smoke-polluted areas. Setts are easily rooted.
Balsam poplars, P. *trichocarpa* Torr. & Gray. P. *tacamahaca* × *trichocarpa* hybrids North America	Often susceptible to a bacterial canker and only clones generally resistant in practice should be used. They withstand slightly more acid soils than the Black hybrids and are more suited to the cooler and wetter parts of Britain than those.		Potential energy crop species grown on very short rotations.		These yields are for plantations established at wide 5–7 m spacings. Higher yields can be obtained by planting the trees more closely together.

Species and native country	Conditions justifying selection	Unsuitable conditions	Notes on timber	General remarks and Yield Class (average YC in brackets)
Birches: Silver birch, *Betula pendula* Roth. Downy birch, *Betula pubescens* Ehrh. British Isles and Europe	Rarely worth planting alone but often useful as nurses for frost-tender conifers or for beech or oak. Prefer light soils in the drier parts of the country including heathland, but these species are ubiquitous as natural growth on felled woodlands.	Should not be planted on any site where they are not clearly wanted for silvicultural reasons or for beauty.	Mainly used in turnery work, e.g. for toys, tool handles and brush backs. Have good strength properties and could find a wider range of uses if grown to saw log size. Pulpwood.	Natural growth is often worth keeping as shelter for a new crop. Must be cut out before it damages the crowns or leaders of more valuable trees. Makes useful firebrooms. 2–10 (4)
English elm, *Ulmus procera* Salis.	Fertile, deep, moist, light loams. Frost hardy. Resists sea winds.	All infertile soils.	Field elm was our most valuable hedgerow timber. Uses include coffin boards, furniture, weather-boarding, box ends, packing-case manufacture, dock piles and fenders. Pulpwood and turnery.	Field elm is usually grown only as a hedgerow tree. Wych elm thrives under forest conditions, particularly in northern and western valleys. Elm hedges and young regrowth unaffected by disease.
Wych elm, *Ulmus glabra* Huds. Britain and Europe	As for English elm. Stands town smoke well. (Elms should not be planted at present because of Dutch elm disease.)	As for English elm.		

Species	Fertile soils / use	Infertile soils / sites	Timber use	Remarks
Limes: *Tilia cordata* Mill. *Tilia platyphyllos* Scop. *Tilia vulgaris* Hayne. Britain and Europe	Fertile soils. Useful as a hedgerow tree to replace elm. Rarely planted, except for amenity.	All infertile soils.	Good for turnery, and is a favourite timber for wood-carving and as pulpwood.	Of limited timber value. Windfirm. Viable seed is produced only rarely.
Norway maple, *Acer platanoides* Europe	Fertile calcareous soils. Useful as a hedgerow tree to replace elm and for planting on chalk downlands.	All infertile soils and exposed sites.	A hard strong smooth-textured wood used for furniture and carving.	Useful amenity tree.
Cricket bat willow, *Salix alba* var. *coerulea* Sm. England	Margins of flowing streams or water courses with alluvial soil or similar highly fertile land.	No good anywhere else.	Used for cricket bats, artificial limbs, chip baskets. Pulpwood.	Growing Cricket bat willows is a highly specialised business.
Gean, or **Wild Cherry,** *Prunus avium* L. Britain and Europe	Fertile woodland soils, particularly over chalk. Useful in mixture with ash, beech or oak.	All infertile soils.	A valuable turnery and furniture wood.	One of the few trees to produce good timber and showy blossoms. Good species to grow if rapid growth assured. Timber can quickly decay when trees become overmature.

Species and native country	Conditions justifying selection	Unsuitable conditions	Notes on timber	General remarks and Yield Class (average YC in brackets)
Red oak, *Quercus borealis* Michx. Eastern North America	Fertile sandy soils.	Very infertile soils.	A general-purpose hardwood with good strength properties. Not a substitute for native oaks.	Valued as an amenity tree because of its autumn colour. Grows rapidly. Nursery treatment resembles common oak. Takes wood preservative well. 4–10 (6)
Southern beeches, *Nothofagus procera* N. obliqua Chile	Reasonably fertile soils in milder localities.	Frost hollows, exposed sites and eastern Britain with colder winters.	Similar to beech but not of such quality. General-purpose hardwood.	Vigorous species, visually attractive trees fitting well into British landscape. Coppices and regenerates well. 10–18
CONIFERS				
Scots pine (SP), *Pinus sylvestris* (L.) British Isles and Northern Europe	An adaptable tree which succeeds over a wide range of conditions. The easiest tree to plant on dry heather sites. Thrives on light or sandy soils and at low or moderate	Avoid soft ground and sites exposed to sea wind. Not easy to establish on moorland country under high rainfall. Unsuitable for chalk or limestone soils. Not a tree for high	A general-purpose timber with good strength properties. It works, nails, and finishes well. Takes preservatives readily so is easily treated for outdoor use. Its wide	Although growth is rather slow and volume production is not high compared with more exacting species, generally it is a 'safe' tree to plant.

Species			
	elevations. Very frost hardy. A strong light-demander. Does well in low-rainfall areas. A useful nurse species.	elevations, except in north-east Scotland, where it thrives up to 500 m in glens.	range of uses includes fencing, joinery, building, flooring, box and packing-case manufacture, pitwood, fibreboard, wood-wool and chipboard manufacture, pulpwood, railway sleepers and telegraph poles. The 'redwood' of the imported timber trade.	4–14 (8)
Corsican pine (CP), *Pinus nigra* var. *maritima* (Ait) Melville Corsica	Low elevations, particularly sandy areas near the sea. Light sandy soils and also heavy clays in the midlands and south and east England; low-rainfall areas. More successful on chalky soils than Scots pine. Tolerates smoke better than other conifers. Useful in mixture with beech.	Avoid high elevations. Not suitable for the northern and western uplands of Britain.	The timber resembles that of Scots pine, but is somewhat coarser in texture, has a higher proportion of sapwood, and has slightly lower strength properties. Readily treated with preservatives. Its other uses include box manufacture, pitwood, fencing, fibreboard manufacture, pulpwood and wood-wool.	Produces timber faster than Scots pine. Shows some tolerance to smoke. More difficult to establish than Scots pine. 6–20 (10)

Species and native country	Conditions justifying selection	Unsuitable conditions	Notes on timber	General remarks and Yield Class (average YC in brackets)
Lodgepole pine (LP), *Pinus contorta* Dougl. ex Loud. Western North America	After suitable ground preparation Lodgepole pine grows relatively well on the poorest heaths, sand-dunes and peat where no other tree will survive. Stands exposure better than most other species. Fairly tolerant of air pollution.	Tends to grow very coarsely on moist fertile sites.	Home-grown timber is used in the round for pitprops and fencing. The sawn timber has similar properties to Scots pine and can be used for the same purposes.	A useful pioneer species in Britain and has been widely planted, especially in the west and north. 4–14 (6)
European larch (EL), *Larix decidua* Mill. Mountains of Central Europe	Site requirements are exacting. Does best on moist but well-drained moderately fertile loams. A strong light-demander. A good nurse tree. Has some tolerance of smoke.	Avoid damp, badly drained or very dry sites, frosty places, shallow soils over chalk, poor sands, peat soils, leached soils, exposed sites at high elevations or near the sea, areas carrying a dense growth of heather.	The timber is heavier and stronger than most other softwoods. The heartwood is naturally durable but any sapwood needs preservatives for outdoor use. It is widely used for fencing, gates, estate work and pitwood. Other uses include telegraph poles, rustic work, garden furniture and chipboard. Selected material is in demand for vat-making, boat-building, and wagons.	Canker is a danger and it is essential to select really suitable sites for planting. Choice of origin of seed for plants is most important; home-collected seed (particularly Scottish), from a good stand, is the most reliable. 4–14 (6)

Species	Suitable sites	Sites to avoid	Timber	Remarks	Yield
Japanese larch (JL), *Larix kaempferi* (Lambert) Carr. Japan	Thrives over a wide range of conditions including the high-rainfall districts of the west and north. Suitable for upland sites including grassy and heathery slopes. Of value in fire belts as it quickly suppresses vegetation. A valuable pioneer species and useful nurse with some resistance to smoke pollution.	Avoid dry sites and areas where the annual rainfall is low (under 30 inches); also badly drained sites, frost hollows and very exposed situations.	The timber is strong and resembles that of European larch. Grade for grade it can be used for the same purposes.	Resistant to larch canker. Gives a higher yield, up to middle age, than European larch or Scots pine.	4–16 (8)
Hybrid larch (HL), *Larix × eurolepis* Henry First raised in Scotland					
Douglas fir (DF), *Pseudotsuga menziesii* (Franco) Mirb. Western North America	Likes a well-drained soil of good depth and of moderate fertility. A tree for valley slopes. Particular care is needed in site selection. A moderate shade bearer for a few years.	Unsuitable for exposed situations, heather ground, wet soils and shallow soils. Liable to windblow on soft ground except where drains are well maintained. Suffers from frost damage when young.	An excellent constructional timber with a high strength-to-weight ratio in compression and bending. Takes preservatives reasonably well. It is used for fencing, pitwood, flooring, joinery, building, packing-case manufacture, telegraph poles, flag poles, chipboard, fibreboard and pulpwood.	On suitable sites Douglas fir grows rapidly and produces a high volume of timber. Thinning at too late a date can render crop unduly susceptible to windblow. Care needed with planting. Excellent conifer for moister, fertile lowland and valley slope sites.	8–24 (14)

Species and native country	Conditions justifying selection	Unsuitable conditions	Notes on timber	General remarks and Yield Class (average YC in brackets)
Norway spruce (NS). *Picea abies* (L.) Karst. Europe	Moist grassy or rushy land, and shallow, less-acid peats. Succeeds on old woodland sites and most soils of moderate fertility including heavy clays. Can withstand light shade for a few years. Somewhat sensitive to exposure.	Fails on uncontrolled heather land and does poorly on dry sites, particularly on the eastern side of Britain. May be checked by frost in hollows and by occasional grazing by roe deer and sheep, but eventually grows away from this.	A good general-purpose timber with a clean white colour. It works and nails well, and has a wide range of uses. It is stable during changing conditions of humidity, and is therefore particularly suitable for building. Its other uses include joinery, kitchen furniture, boxes and packing-cases, pulpwood, chipboard, pitwood, fencing, fibreboard, wood-wool, ladder poles and scaffold poles. The 'whitewood' of the imported timber trade. Seldom used out of doors. Small poles take enough preservative to use as fence-posts.	Where it is really at home, Norway spruce produces a high volume of timber. Good drainage is essential if windblow is to be avoided. The young trees, and often tops of thinnings, can be sold as Christmas trees, but only in November/December. 6–22 (12)

Sitka spruce (SS), *Picea sitchensis* (Bong.) Carr. Western North America	Damp sites, generally, including exposed high land. Stands exposure better than any other common conifer, very suitable for high-rainfall districts especially on the west coast.	Avoid all dry sites. Not a tree for the dry east nor for southern and midland England. Can suffer severe damage from frost when young and check on uncontrolled heather.	Properties and uses are similar to those of Norway spruce. A first-class pulpwood and readily accepted for chipboard, boxboards and many building jobs but not for high-grade joinery.	A faster grower than Norway spruce and very large volume producer. Useless as Christmas tree. Wide provenance variation. Queen Charlotte Island (B.C.) is a safe choice but on southern sites Washington and Oregon are preferred. Britain's most widely planted conifer. 6–24 (12)
Lawson cypress (LC), *Chamaecyparis lawsoniana* (A. Marr.) Parl. Western North America	Soil requirements are not exacting, but does best on a deep fertile soil preferably in a sheltered situation. Stands shade well, is fairly frost hardy, and is sometimes of value in areas associated with chalk.	Avoid heather ground	There is too little home-grown timber of this species on the market for it to be considered for any special purpose. It finds an outlet as a general-purpose softwood.	Of limited value; has a tendency to fork and is liable to suffer from snow break. Foliage is valued by florists. Widely used as hedging. 12–24 (14)

Other conifers.
Many other species grow well in Britain including Western hemlock, Western red cedar, Grand fir, Noble fir, the redwoods, and several other pines. They are unlikely to find widespread use in farm planting though may be useful for specific situations e.g. Radiata pine (*Pinus radiata*) on exposed coastal plantings or Western red cedar as a conifer nurse on chalky soils.

APPENDIX 2

CHAPTER REFERENCES FOR FURTHER READING AND
OTHER INFORMATION

Chapter 1

Small Woods on Farms, Countryside Commission booklet **CCP143**, 1983.
Peterken, G. F., 1981, *Woodland Conservation and Management*, Chapman
   & Hall.
The Potential for Forestry on the Culm Measures of South-west England,
   Dartington Institute, 1986.
Harris, E. & J., 1981, *The Guinness Book of Trees*.
Insley, H., 1988, *Farm Woodland Planning*, Forestry Commission Bulletin 80.
Richards, E. G., 1988, *Trees as a Farm Crop*, Blackwell.

Chapter 2

Practical Work in Farm Woods. A series of eight leaflets published jointly by
ADAS and the Forestry Commission. A4 format. Free. 1986:
   1. 'Why Manage Farm Woods?' (P3017)
   2. 'Woodland Survey and Assessment' (P3018)
   3. 'Management for Wood Production' (P3019)
   4. 'Woodland and Farm Resources' (P3020)
   5. 'Woodland Management for Wildlife and Landscape Conservation'
      (P3021)
   6. 'Woodland Management for Sport and Recreation' (P3022)
   7. 'New Planting' (P3023)
   8. 'Woodland Operations' (P3024).

Forestry Practice, Forestry Commission bulletin **14**, HMSO (regularly revised
   and updated).
Silviculture of Broadleaved Woodland, Forestry Commission bulletin **62**,
   HMSO, 1984.
Coppice, Forestry Commission leaflet **83** HMSO (2nd edn), 1986.
Small Woods on Farms, Countryside Commission booklet **CCP 143**, 1983.

Chapter 4

Several titles listed for Chapter 2 are relevant but the following will also be found useful:

Hart, C. E., 1987, *Private Woodlands: A guide to British timber prices and forestry costings*. Obtainable from the author: Chenies, Coleford, Glos. GL16 8DT.

Savill, P. S. and Evans, J., 1986, *Plantation Silviculture in Temperate Regions with Special Reference to the British Isles*, Oxford.

The Use of Herbicides in the Forest, Forestry Commission field book 8, 1989 (regularly updated).

Forestry Fencing, Forestry Commission leaflet **87**, 1986.

Hibberd, B. G. (ed.), 1988, *Farm Woodland Practice*, Forestry Commission Handbook No. 3.

Chapter 6

1949   National Parks and Access to the Countryside Act
1967   Countryside (Scotland) Act
1968   Countryside Act
1973   Nature Conservancy Council Act
1981   Wildlife and Countryside Act
1981   Countryside Scotland Act.

Chapter 7

Leaflet on Farm Woodland Scheme is *Farming and Rural Enterprises*, HMSO (1987).
External signs of decay in trees, Forestry Commission arboricultural leaflet **1**, HMSO (2nd edn), 1985.

Chapter 8

Forestry Commission Publications, HMSO:
  Mid-Diameter Sawlog Tables,   booklet 26
  Forest Mensuration Handbook,   booklet 39
  Yield Models for Forest Management,   booklet 48
  Thinning Control,   field book 2
  Forestry Practice (10th edn, 1986),   bulletin 14
Hart, C. E., 1987, *Private Woodlands: A guide to British timber prices and forestry costings*. Obtainable from the author: Chenies, Coleford, Glos. GL16 8DT.

Chapter 9

The Interaction of Forestry and Farming, Mutch, W. E. S. and Hutchison, A. R., 1979, University of Edinburgh.

The Hill Farming Research Organisation, *Biennial Report*, 1979–81.
Farming Trees: the case for government support for woodland on farms, an NFU policy document, 1986.

Chapter 10

James, N. D. G. (3rd edn), 1982, *The Forester's Companion*, Blackwell.
Forestry Safety Council leaflets (free), Forestry Commission, 231 Corstorphine Road, Edinburgh EH12 7AT.

Trade Journals
Forestry and British Timber (monthly). Benn Publications Ltd, Sovereign Way, Tonbridge, Kent TN9 1RW.
Timber Grower (quarterly), Timber Growers United Kingdom Ltd. (TGUK), 5 Dublin Street Lane South, Edinburgh EH1 3PX.
Agriculture House, Knightsbridge, London SW1X 7NJ.

Forestry Suppliers
Forestry and British Timber Directory, annual guide to forestry products, suppliers and services. Benn Publications Ltd, Sovereign Way, Tonbridge, Kent TN9 1RW.

Also see Trade Journals and Yellow Pages under 'Tree Work'.

APPENDIX 3

Agricultural Development and Advisory Service (ADAS)

HQ Great Westminster House
   Horseferry Road
   London SW1P 2AE.

   (071 238 3000)

ADAS
Nobel House
17 Smith Square
London SW1P 3JR.

(For *local office*, see phone book.)

Agricultural Training Board

England
Summit House
Glebe Way
West Wickham
Kent BR4 0RF.

(081 777 9003)

Scotland
Overgogar House
Gogar Bank
Edinburgh EH12 9DD.

(031 339 3002)

Arboricultural Association

Ampfield House
Ampfield
Near Romsey
Hants SO5 9PA.

(0794 68717)

Specialists in individual trees and clumps for amenity. Keep a register of tree surveyors.

British Association for Shooting and Conservation

Marford Mill
Rosset
Wrexham
Clwyd LL12 0HL.

(0244 570881)

Scotland
Trochry
By Dunkeld

(03503 226)

British Timber Merchants' Association

Stocking Lane
Hughenden Valley
High Wycombe
Bucks HP14 4JZ.

(024024 3602)

British Trust for Conservation Volunteers

36 St. Mary's Street
Wallingford
Oxon OX10 0EU.

(0491 39766)

Council for National Parks

45 Shelton Street
London WC2H 9HJ.

(071 240 3603)

Country Landowners Association

16 Belgrave Square
London SW1X 8PQ.

(071 235 0511)

Countryside Commission

John Dower House
Crescent Place
Cheltenham GL50 3RA.

(0242 521381)

Countryside Council for Wales

Plas Penrhos
Ffordd Penrhos
Bangor
Gwynedd LL57 2LQ.

(0248 370444)

Countryside Commission for Scotland

Battleby
Redgorton
Perthshire PH1 3EW.

(0738 27921)

County/Regional Planning Authorities

See phone book for local council offices

Farming and Wildlife Advisory Trust

National Agricultural Centre
Stoneleigh
Kenilworth
Warwickshire CV8 2RX.

(0203 696699)

Forestry Commission

HQ 231 Corstorphine Road
   Edinburgh EH12 7AT.

   (031 334 0303)

Regional Offices

N England

1a Grosvenor Terrace
York YO3 7BD.

(0904 620221)

N Scotland

21 Church Street
Inverness IV1 1EL.

(0463 232811)

Wales

Victoria Terrace
Aberystwyth
Dyfed SY23 2DQ.

(0970 612367)

E England

Gt. Eastern House
Tenison Road
Cambridge CB1 2DU.

(0223 314546)

Mid Scotland

Portcullis House
21 India Street
Glasgow G2 4PL.

(041 248 3931)

W England

Avon Fields House
Somerdale
Keynsham
Bristol BS18 2BD.

(0272 869481)

S Scotland

55/57 Moffat Road
Dumfries DG1 1NP.

(0387 69171)

Research Stations

Alice Holt Lodge
Wrecclesham
Farnham
Surrey GU10 4LH

(0420 22255)

F.C. Northern Research Station
Roslin
Midlothian EH25 9SY

(031 445 2176)

Forestry Safety Council   *Forestry Training Council*

231 Corstorphine Road   231 Corstorphine Road
Edinburgh EH12 7AT.   Edinburgh EH12 7AT.

(031 334 0303)   (031 334 0303)

The Game Conservancy Ltd

Burgate Manor
Fordingbridge
Hants SP6 1EF.

(0425 52381)

Institute of Chartered Foresters

22 Walker Street   Keep a register of professional forestry
Edinburgh EH3 7HR.   consultants

(031 225 2705)

Ministry of Agriculture Fisheries and Food

Whitehall Place
London SW1A 2HH

(071 270 3000)

National Farmers' Union   *National Farmers' Union of Scotland*

Agriculture House   17 Grosvenor Crescent
25–31 Knightsbridge   Edinburgh EH12 5EN
London SW1X 7NJ.
                                   (031 337 4333)
(071 235 5077)

(For *local offices* see phone book.)

Nature Conservancy Council for England

Northminster House
Peterborough PE1 1UA.

(0733 40345)

Nature Conservancy Council for Scotland

12 Hope Terrace
Edinburgh EH9 2AS.

(031 447 4784)

Countryside Council for Wales

Plas Penrhos
Ffordd Penrhos
Bangor
Gwynedd LL57 2LQ.

(0248 370444)

(For *local offices* see phone book.)

Royal Forestry Society
102 High Street
Tring
Herts HP23 4AF.

(0442 822028)

Royal Institute of Chartered Surveyors

England

12 Great George Street
Parliament Square
London SW1P 3AD.

(071 222 7000)

Scotland

9 Manor Place
Edinburgh EH3 7DN.

(031 225 7078)

Royal Scottish Forestry Society

11 Atholl Crescent
Edinburgh EH3 8HE.

(031 229 8180) or (031 229 1212)

Scottish Agricultural College

Headquarters

Cleeve Gardens
Oakbank Road
Perth PH1 1HF.

(0738) 36611

581 King Street
Aberdeen AB9 1UD.

(0224 480291)

Auchincruive
Ayr KA6 5HW.

(0292 520331)

West Mains Road
Edinburgh EH9 3JG.

(031 667 1041)

Scottish Landowners' Federation

25 Maritime Street
Edinburgh EH6 5PW.

(031 555 1031)

Scottish Office Agriculture and Fisheries Department

Pentland House
47 Robbs Loan
Edinburgh EH14 1TW

(031 556 8400)

Timber Growers' (UK) Ltd

Adanel House
24 High Street
Wimbledon
London SW19 5DX.

(081 944 6340)

Scottish HQ

5 Dublin Street Lane South
Edinburgh EH1 3PX.

(031 557 0944)

Welsh Office Department of Agriculture

Park Avenue
Aberystwyth
Dyfed SY23 1PQ.

(0970 615022)

The Woodland Trust

Autumn Park
Dysart Road
Grantham
Lincs NG31 6LL.

(0476 74297)

Scottish HQ

54 Manor Place
Edinburgh EH3 7EH.
(031 225 3543)

INDEX

Figures in italics refer to illustrations or tables

192